WORLD HISTORY SERIES ■ ■ ■

The Mongol Empire

Titles in the World History Series

WORLD HISTORY SERIES ■ ■ ■

The Mongol Empire

by
Mary Hull

Lucent Books, P.O. Box 289011, San Diego, CA 92198-9011

Library of Congress Cataloging-in-Publication Data

Hull, Mary.
    The Mongol empire / by Mary Hull.
        p. cm.—(World history series)
    Includes bibliographical references and index.
    Summary: A historical overview of the rise of the Mongol
Empire in Asia, its effects, and its legacy.
    ISBN 1-56006-312-2   (alk. paper)
    1. Mongols—History—Juvenile literature.   [1. Mongols—
History.]   I. Title. II. Series.
DS19.H877   1998
951'.025—dc21   97-29991
                                                                        CIP
                                                                         AC

Copyright 1998 by Lucent Books, Inc., P.O. Box 289011,
San Diego, California 92198-9011

Printed in the U.S.A.

Contents

Foreword

Each year on the first day of school, nearly every history teacher faces the task of explaining why his or her students should study history. One logical answer to this question is that exploring what happened in our past explains how the things we often take for granted—our customs, ideas, and institutions—came to be. As statesman and historian Winston Churchill put it, "Every nation or group of nations has its own tale to tell. Knowledge of the trials and struggles is necessary to all who would comprehend the problems, perils, challenges, and opportunities which confront us today." Thus, a study of history puts modern ideas and institutions in perspective. For example, though the founders of the United States were talented and creative thinkers, they clearly did not invent the concept of democracy. Instead, they adapted some democratic ideas that had originated in ancient Greece and with which the Romans, the British, and others had experimented. An exploration of these cultures, then, reveals their very real connection to us through institutions that continue to shape our daily lives.

Another reason often given for studying history is the idea that lessons exist in the past from which contemporary societies can benefit and learn. This idea, although controversial, has always been an intriguing one for historians. Those who agree that society can benefit from the past often quote philosopher George Santayana's famous statement, "Those who cannot remember the past are condemned to repeat it." Historians who ascribe to Santayana's philosophy believe that, for example, studying the events that led up to the major world wars or other significant historical events would allow society to chart a different and more favorable course in the future.

Just as difficult as convincing students to realize the importance of studying history is the search for useful and interesting supplementary materials that present historical events in a context that can be easily understood. The volumes in Lucent Books' World History Series attempt to present a broad, balanced, and penetrating view of the march of history. Ancient Egypt's important wars and rulers, for example, are presented against the rich and colorful backdrop of Egyptian religious, social, and cultural developments. The series engages the reader by enhancing historical events with these cultural contexts. For example, in *Ancient Greece*, the text covers the role of women in that society. Slavery is discussed in *The Roman Empire*, as well as how slaves earned their freedom. The numerous and varied aspects of everyday life in these and other societies are explored in each volume of the series. Additionally, the series covers the major political, cultural, and philosophical ideas as the torch of civilization is passed from ancient Mesopotamia and Egypt, through Greece, Rome, Medieval Europe, and other world cultures, to the modern day.

The material in the series is formatted in a thorough, precise, and organized manner. Each volume offers the reader a comprehensive and clearly written overview of an important historical event or period. The topic under discussion is placed in a broad historical context. For example, *The Italian Renaissance* begins with a discussion of the High Middle Ages and the loss of central control that allowed certain Italian cities to develop artistically. The book ends by looking forward to the Reformation and interpreting the societal changes that grew out of the Renaissance. Thus, students are not only involved in an historical era, but also enveloped by the events leading up to that era and the events following it.

One important and unique feature in the World History Series is the primary and secondary source quotations that richly supplement each volume. These quotes are useful in a number of ways. First, they allow students access to sources they would not normally be exposed to because of the difficulty and obscurity of the original source. The quotations range from interesting anecdotes to farsighted cultural perspectives and are drawn from historical witnesses both past and present. Second, the quotes demonstrate how and where historians themselves derive their information on the past as they strive to reach a consensus on historical events. Lastly, all of the quotes are footnoted, familiarizing students with the citation process and allowing them to verify quotes and/or look up the original source if the quote piques their interest.

Finally, the books in the World History Series provide a detailed launching point for further research. Each book contains a bibliography specifically geared toward student research. A second, annotated bibliography introduces students to all the sources the author consulted when compiling the book. A chronology of important dates gives students an overview, at a glance, of the topic covered. Where applicable, a glossary of terms is included.

In short, the series is designed not only to acquaint readers with the basics of history, but also to make them aware that their lives are a part of an ongoing human saga. Perhaps they will then come to the same realization as famed historian Arnold Toynbee. In his monumental work, *A Study of History*, he wrote about becoming aware of history flowing through him in a mighty current, and of his own life "welling like a wave in the flow of this vast tide."

Important Dates in the History of the Mongol Empire

ca. 1167	1180	1193	1206	1219	1232	1245	1258

ca. 1167
Genghis Khan is born

1206
Genghis Khan is declared leader of all the tribes at a *quriltai* in Mongolia

1211
Mongols invade the Chin Empire in northern China

1218
Genghis Khan invades the empire of the Khwarazm Shah

1227
Genghis Khan dies

1229
Ogodei is declared Great Khan

1235
Ogodei Khan's Mongol capital at Karakorum is completed

1237–1242
Batu campaigns in Russia and eastern Europe

1241
Battle of the River Sajo; Ogodei Khan dies

1245–1247
Friar Giovanni of Plano Carpini journeys to Mongolia

1246
Guyuk Khan is elected

1248
Guyuk Khan dies

1251
Mongke Khan is elected

1252
Campaigns against Sung China begin

1253–1255
Friar William of Rubruck travels to Mongolia

1255
Hulagu begins Persian campaign

1255
Batu, khan of the Golden Horde, dies

1257
Berke succeeds as khan of the Golden Horde

1258
Baghdad falls to Hulagu; the Abbasid dynasty is finished

1259
Mongke Khan dies

1260
Kubilai and his brother Ariq Boke are both elected Great Khan at different *quriltais*, touching off a civil war

1261–1262
Civil war erupts between Hulagu and Berke Khan

1264
Kubilai defeats Ariq Boke

1265
Hulagu, khan of the Ilkhanate, dies

1266
Kubilai constructs a new Mongol capital, Ta-tu, in China

1267
Berke, khan of the Golden Horde, dies

1274
Kubilai Khan leads a failed expedition against Japan

1279
The Sung Empire is defeated in China

1281
A second Mongol expedition against Japan fails

1294
Kubilai Khan dies

1295
The Ilkhanate embraces Islam

1345
Outbreak of the plague among the Mongol force besieging Kaffa; this plague, the Black Death, spreads to Europe

1353–1354
The Black Death reaches China

1368
The Mongols are driven from China by the Ming

A Force from the East

In the thirteenth century, a tribe of people living in eastern Mongolia rose from obscurity to the forefront of international affairs. Uniting with other tribes of the steppe, they formed a powerful army under the leadership of a man known as Genghis Khan. By 1260, the conquests of Genghis Khan's army had led to the formation of the Mongol Empire, which ruled two-thirds of the Eurasian landmass, including all of present-day China, Mongolia, Iran, Iraq, Afghanistan, Korea, and parts of modern Siberia, Russia, Turkey, Syria, Pakistan, India, Vietnam, and Cambodia. Genghis Khan conquered more territory with his armies than any other individual in world history.

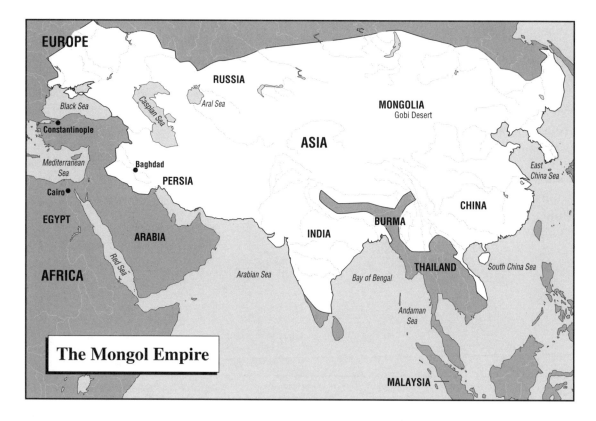

The Mongol Empire

Under the strong leadership of Genghis Khan, the Mongols established one of the largest empires in world history.

By 1280, under the leadership of Genghis's descendants, Mongol rule extended from the Mediterranean to the Yellow Sea. At its height, the Mongol Empire was exceeded in size and scope only by the British Empire of the nineteenth century. And though some of the empire's hordes (regions ruled by subordinate khans who deferred to the Great Khan) eventually became independent kingdoms, they managed to survive long after the collapse of the empire. The Golden Horde in Russia, which had originally been ruled by Genghis's brother Batu Khan, lasted until 1502, when it was annexed by Catherine the Great. Descendants of the Mongols also began the Moghul Empire in India, which lasted well into the sixteenth century. In the centuries following its collapse, the Mongol Empire continued to leave its mark on the political structures of eastern Europe, Asia, and the Middle East.

The transformation of the Mongols from a nomadic tribe to a world power with conquests that surpassed those of the Roman Empire was nothing short of amazing. At the end of the twelfth century, the Mongols were just one of many minor nomadic tribes who constantly quarreled among each other on the steppe. Sometimes they banded together to conduct a raid or defend themselves against danger, but their associations were never stable. Alliances shifted frequently, and coalitions were always temporary. The steppe tribes had never consolidated to form a stable or lasting unified force prior to Genghis Khan.

The Pax Mongolica

The Mongol tribe seemed an unlikely group to produce one of the world's greatest leaders, but Genghis Khan, the son of a herdsman from the farthest reaches of Mongolia, was able to transform the feuding steppe tribes into a powerful nation and construct an army that became the most accomplished and technological force of its time. With this army, Genghis and his descendants created an empire that would affect the course of history. By bringing so many disparate countries together under the rule of one Mongol empire, Genghis Khan linked the eastern and western worlds in unprecedented ways.

Under the Pax Mongolica, a period of relative peace inspired by the control of so many lands under one authority, overland travel from Europe to Asia became much safer. Trade routes flourished under Mongol rule, and cultural exchange was promoted through the spread of individuals, goods, and ideas. The Mongols brought Persian doctors and astronomers together with their Chinese counterparts, and this collaboration helped advance medicine and other scientific knowledge. European missionaries and merchants traveled to the Mongol Empire and brought back valuable information about Asian geography and culture that sparked a new generation of explorers. Christopher Columbus, for example, was inspired to sail west after reading the Venetian traveler Marco Polo's account of the Mongol Empire. Believing he would reach the Mongols, Columbus was carrying letters addressed to the "Khan of Cathay" and a dog-eared copy of Polo's *A Description of the World* when he encountered the New World.

The cultural exchanges brought about by the Pax Mongolica had far-reaching consequences for all parts of the globe. An obscure tribe of people from the farthest reaches of Mongolia had created a vast empire that would affect the course of history. The Mongols, who gathered talented fighters and leaders, managed to build and administrate an empire that left its mark—culturally, technologically, and politically—on the world.

1 The Nine-Tongued People

There was a blue wolf which was born having his destiny from heaven above. His spouse was a fallow doe. They came, passing over the Sea. Batacaciqan was born when they camped at the head of the Onon River, at Mount Burkhan Qaldun.

The Secret History of the Mongols

Batacaciqan, the son of the wolf and the deer, was the mythological ancestor of the Mongol tribe, which banded together with other warlike tribes that had lived, since early human history, in the region known as Mongolia. In the twelfth century, Mongolia was inhabited by roughly thirty nomadic tribes comprising a population between 1.5 and 3 million people. These different tribes were related linguistically but between them spoke nine Turkic, Tungusic, and Mongolic variants of the Altaic language, named for the Altai Mountains that make up the western border of the region in which they lived. Known as the steppe, the homeland of these tribes was a vast, level, and largely treeless tract of land that stretched across Asia. The different steppe tribes were not yet collectively known as "Mongols." Lacking a collective identity, the tribes called themselves the "Felt-Tented Nations," or, as a reflection of their linguistic diversity, the "Nine-Tongued People." But each tribe had its own name. The Mongol group, whose members would emerge as leaders and whose name would become synonymous with all the people of the steppe, had their origin in the forested northwest country.

Life Among the Nomads

Much of the land in Mongolia was unsuitable for agriculture. And because the steppe tribes had no agriculture, there was no food surplus, causing their populations to be very low for a region that was so vast, comprising nearly 380 million acres.

Each tribe spread out in smaller encampments within the steppe. Thus the Mongol tribe was made up of many smaller clans that were dispersed over a wide territory. Each clan—an extended family that included a man, his wives, brothers, children, and grandchildren—might have its own camp. Before Genghis Khan's rise to power, the tribes had no central authority or leader. Clans and tribes might form a temporary alliance with a powerful figure, but these loyalties shifted frequently. The tribes lived near flat, open pastures in the summer and moved to protected river valleys in the winter.

A modern nomadic family relocates its home on the Mongolian steppe. Today, nomadic peoples continue to inhabit the barren steppe, just as in the days of Genghis Khan.

The Mongol Herds

To sustain themselves, the tribes maintained herds of grazing animals such as horses, sheep, goats, and cattle. They migrated seasonally in order to find suitable grazing grounds for their horses and herds. Each tribe or clan had its favored grazing grounds, which it returned to in the summer; maintaining control over pasturelands was a frequent source of conflict between the tribes.

Horses were essential to the Mongols, and to all of the steppe tribes. Domesticated in southern Russia as early as the second millennium B.C., horses provided a primary mode of transport. Horses also helped the steppe tribes to tend their herds and to hunt. In addition, the Mongols used mares' milk to create a favorite alcoholic beverage called *koumiss.*

Other animals commonly used by the nomads were cattle, which made good pack animals and could be slaughtered for their beef, and sheep and goats, which provided the staples of their diet—meat, milk, and cheese.

Each fall a Mongol family would slaughter some of its sheep and freeze the mutton by burying it in the ground. The Mongolian steppe has always been subject to great extremes in temperature, from 104 degrees Fahrenheit in summer to -40 degrees in winter. Although the steppe is a grassy plain all summer, from November to April of each year the ground is frozen. During the winter, frozen slabs of mutton would be boiled with blocks of ice cut from frozen rivers or lakes to produce a stew that provided the Mongols' main source of protein.

Meat was usually boiled or roasted; it would only be eaten raw under extreme circumstances, such as the inability to make a fire. Sometimes meat was tenderized by placing it under the saddle of a horse or camel that was ridden all day. Some foreigners who encountered the Mongols were repulsed by their eating habits. According to Giovanni of Plano Carpini, a Dominican friar sent to make religious overtures to the tribe in the mid-thirteenth century, the Mongols were not fastidious in their eating habits.

> Their food consists of everything that can be eaten, for they eat dogs, wolves, foxes, and horses, and when driven by necessity, they feed on human flesh. They eat the filth which comes away from mares when they bring forth foals. Nay, I have seen them eating lice. They would say, "Why should I not eat them since they eat the flesh of my son and drink his blood?" I have also seen them eat mice.[1]

The young men of the clan were given the best and richest food, while the older people ate what was left over. Although older people were respected for their advice and counsel, the best food went to the young because they were responsible for protecting the tribe. Everyone in the household ate from a common pot. Friar Carpini described how "one of them cuts the morsels and another takes them on the point of a knife and offers them to each, to some more, to some less, according to whether they wish to show them greater or less honor."[2]

The Felt Tent

In addition to food, sheep also provided wool, which could be used to make heavy-duty cloth. The nomads manufactured felt

A Mongol shepherd tends to his herds of cattle, sheep, and goats. These herds, along with their by-products of milk and cheese, constituted the staples of the ancient Mongols' diet.

from sheep's wool by beating strips of wet wool together, then tying them to horses' tails, where the fibers would be dragged over the ground, tangling them together. Felt was then coated with tallow to make it waterproof. It was used for a variety of purposes, such as being sewn into a waterproof cloak. But one of the most important uses of felt was as a cover for Mongol homes.

A Mongol family lived in a six-sided or round home called a *yurt,* or *ger.* These homes could be dismantled and loaded onto a cart in less than an hour, which was suitable for a nomadic lifestyle. The yurt consisted of a lightweight wooden frame covered with a layer of sturdy felt to keep out the wind and rain. The doors of the yurts always faced south to avoid the cold west and north winds. Planking was often laid down on the floor, and beds, cupboards, and chests containing treasured objects were arranged in a circle around the wall. Each yurt had a hearth in the center, where dried dung would be used to make a fire. The smoke rose through a hole made in the roof. Mongol women were responsible for gathering dung and making fires.

Mongol Women

Mongol women were married at a young age, often to a man of their parents' choosing. Parents often arranged marriages between their children while they were still quite young, as a means of affirming an alliance. A young Mongol man might be allowed to choose his wife from among the girls of a certain tribe selected by his parents. Since steppe nomads would

Mongols lived in felt tents called yurts. These sturdy yet lightweight homes could be quickly dismantled and loaded onto carts when a clan moved its camp.

take as many wives as they could afford, women sometimes shared a husband. Friar Carpini described the Mongols' practice of polygamy:

> Each man had as many wives as he can keep, one a hundred, another fifty, another ten—one more, another less. It is the general custom for them to marry any of their relations, with the exception of their mother, daughter and sister by the same mother. They can however take in marriage their sisters who have only the same father, and even their father's wives after his death; also a younger brother may marry his brother's wife after his death; or another younger relation is expected to take her. All other women they take as wives without any distinction and they buy them at a very high price from their parents.[3]

Female Strength and Ruggedness

Wives were often trusted political advisers to their husbands, and Mongol women were known for taking charge in their husbands' absence. If their husbands were going on extended campaigns, the women would pack the family belongings and follow behind them, making camp as they went along. And during campaigns, when the battles were over, Mongol women would go to the battlefield and kill the wounded enemy.

To foreigners who were not accustomed to women exhibiting such fortitude, the strength and ruggedness of Mongol women was often jarring. Friar Carpini wrote, "Young girls and women ride and

A modern Mongol woman, dressed in the fashion of her ancestors, stands in the stark Gobi Desert. She holds a rake for collecting dung, which she uses as fuel to heat her yurt.

gallop on horseback with agility like the men. We even saw them carrying bows and arrows. Both the men and the women are able to endure long stretches of riding."[4]

Another European friar, William of Rubruck, who traveled to Mongol lands in 1253, recorded that the women rode astride the horses like men, tying a strip of cloth around their chest to bind their breasts before riding. He also noted that women loaded and unloaded the yurts onto carts and drove the carts when the clan moved.

Mongol women also had a host of other responsibilities. They milked the cows and made butter and *grut* (sour curds). They dressed animal skins and sewed them with thread made from tendons to make leather tunics, shoes, leggings, and other garments. In addition, it was the women who prepared (most of) the meals.

There were some chores no Mongol would perform. The Mongols did not wash their clothes or pots because they believed that the water was a live spirit and that to pollute it would be sinful. According to Friar Rubruck:

> They never wash their clothes, for they say that it makes God angry and that it would thunder if they hung them out to dry; they even beat those who do wash them and take them away from them. They are extraordinarily afraid of thunder. At such a time they turn all strangers out of their dwellings and wrap themselves up in black felt in which they hide until it has passed over.[5]

Similarly, they had rules that prevented them from bathing or urinating in running water, acts they believed offended the spirits.

Mongol Shamanism

The Mongols practiced shamanism, a religion common in the Ural and Altaic mountain areas of northern Asia and Europe. Shamanists believe in an unseen world of gods, ancestral spirits, and demons that can influence the course of events. Spirits abound in shamanism, and spirits live in mountains, woods, rivers, stones, and animals.

The Mongols' supreme god, Tengri, lived in the sky and was called the Eternal Blue Heaven. To speak to the Eternal Blue Heaven, the Mongols climbed to the top of sacred mountains and humbled themselves. Shamans, or holy men and women, had a magic that gave them access to this world of spirits. Like soothsayers, shamans divined the future, often by consulting oracle bones—the burned shoulder blades of sheep—and interpreting the cracks and lines that formed. Shamans were frequently consulted to interpret events or to predict which day was the best to set out on a journey or begin an undertaking. Because Shamanism did not involve public worship of any kind, and because the Mongols were extremely tolerant of other religions, many foreigners believed the Mongols did not have any religion at all.

Technology

Life was simple on the steppe, and Mongol technology was not sophisticated; the tribes made wooden carts and wheels and practiced simple metal work to make weapons and tools. Men made bows, arrows, and arrowheads, as well as saddles and leather bags. If they desired something they could not make themselves, the nomads traded and sometimes stole from adjacent settled societies. Occasionally bands of horsemen would raid a Chinese village and cart off the women, animals, and wares. The Mongols were especially fond of material goods they were unable to produce like silk, silver, and gold. While they usually made their living as herdsmen and hunters, on occasion they would take up arms and go on plundering expeditions into rich Chinese lands.

For centuries, bands of nomadic horsemen had ridden out of Mongolia and plundered neighboring Chinese villages and towns. The Chinese derisively referred to these rough horsemen as the "uncooked." The Chinese were not threatened by the raids, however, for the nomads had no desire to conquer and govern a sedentary agricultural nation like China. As nomads, the Mongols considered

---

The Abduction of Cai Yan

In 192 B.C. a raiding party of steppe nomads invaded a Chinese village and captured a woman named Cai Yan, who was known for her scholarship and poetry. Cai Yan was forced to marry a steppe chieftain and live among the nomads, whose lifestyle she despised. After bearing her new husband two sons, Cai Yan was eventually ransomed by the Chinese and forced to leave her sons behind when she rejoined her people. Cai Yan wrote a poetic composition, titled "Eighteen Songs of a Nomad Flute," that describes her life among the "barbarians," as she referred to the people of the steppe.

A barbarian of the northwest tribes took me to wife by force,
He led me on a journey to the lands at the horizon,
Ten thousand strata of cloudy peaks, so stretched the returning road,
A thousand miles of piercing winds, driving dust and sand.
The people extravagantly savage, violent—like reptiles and snakes,
They draw their bows, they wear armor, their bearing arrogant and fierce. . . . My will shattered, my heart broken, I lament and sigh.
I traveled across the land of Han and entered barbarian domains,
My home was lost, my body violated; better never to have been born.
The felts and furs they make into clothes are a shock to my bones and flesh, I cannot hide my disgust for the taste of their rank-smelling mutton. War drums pulse through the night until it grows light. . . .
I do not know if there is someone to share my grieving heart.
The border wastes are desolate, ten thousand miles of beacons,
Their customs despise the old and the weak, in favor of the young and strong. They wander wherever water and grass may be, and there set up camps and defenses. Cattle and sheep seem to fill the land, swarming like bees or ants. When the grass is finished and water used up, livestock and horses all move. . . . I hate living in this place!

themselves superior to all settled peoples and other ways of life. Although the steppe nomads lived next to the Chinese at a time when Chinese culture was pervading most of east Asia, they rejected Chinese customs and ways of life.

The Chinese kept an eye on the tribes and tried to form relationships with the most powerful ones. Beginning about 200 B.C., official Chinese court historians recorded the names of dangerous and aggressive tribes who had posed military threats. Known as the "Hsiung-nu" in these records, the nomads were considered a nuisance throughout the centuries.

To avoid attack, the Chinese would bribe the most powerful of the steppe tribes and encourage them to aggravate the other groups. Using this "divide and conquer" logic, the Chinese helped create disharmony among the tribes and kept them quarreling with the hope that by promoting conflicts they could prevent the steppe tribes from ever uniting and posing a serious threat to China. The Chinese policy toward the nomads worked until the twelfth century.

Quarreling Tribes

In the twelfth century, the most powerful of the steppe tribes were the Tartars, the Kereyids, the Merkits, and the Naimans. Their continuous tribal warfare wreaked havoc on the steppe lifestyle. Horses were stolen; sheep herds were also taken and

How the Mongols Appeared to Others

Prejevalsky, a Russian soldier who traveled in Mongolia in the nineteenth century, left the following description of the Mongols, recorded in Malcom Yapp's Genghis Khan and the Mongol Empire.

"A broad flat face, with high cheek bones, wide nostrils, small narrow eyes, large prominent ears, coarse black hair, scanty whiskers and beard, a dark sunburnt complexion, and, lastly, a stout thickset figure, rather above average height: such are the distinguishing features of this race.

The first thing which strikes the traveller in the life of the Mongol is his excessive dirtiness: he never washes his body, and very seldom his face and hands. Owing to constant dirt, his clothing swarms with parasites, which he amuses himself by killing in the most unceremonious way. It is a common sight to see a Mongol open his sheepskin or kaftan to catch an offending insect and execute him on the spot between his front teeth. The uncleanliness and dirt amidst which they live is partly attributable to their dislike, almost amounting to dread, of water or damp."

A Tartar warrior brandishes a sword. During the twelfth century the belligerent Tartars were one of the most powerful tribes on the steppe.

slaughtered. Because the tribes were constantly warring, they lived in utter poverty.

As the shaman Teb-Tengri later told the descendants of Genghis Khan:

> Before you were born the stars turned in the heavens. Everyone was feuding. Rather than sleep they robbed each other of their possessions. The earth and its crust had moved. The whole nation was in rebellion. Rather than rest,

they fought each other. In such a world one did not live as one wished, but rather in constant conflict. There was no respite, only battle. There was no affection, only mutual slaughter.[6]

In this period of unrest and instability on the steppe, morals declined, and acts of robbery, rape, and other violence against the traditional nomads' code became symbols of superiority and power. This breakdown of moral codes caused the clan order, which was the basis for Mongol society, to deteriorate. Rashid ad-Din, a Persian chronicler, recorded this saying from the Mongols:

> When in a tribe the sons do not heed the teachings of their fathers and the younger sons do not listen to the words of the elder sons, the husband has no trust in his wife and the wife does not obey the orders of her husband, the father-in-law does not approve of his daughters-in-law and these show no respect for their father-in-law, the great do not protect the common people, and the latter do not obey the instructions of their superiors, . . . in such a tribe the robbers, the liars, the evil-doers, the good-for-nothings [will become so numerous that they] will overshadow the sun itself.[7]

During this time, young men began to abandon their clans to enter the service of any leader who could provide for them. Called *nokhod*, or "followers," these men lived in their leader's household and were supported by him. In exchange, they helped their leader in war, protected him from the enemy, and performed household chores. *Nokhod* were rewarded with a share in the plunder of war; they lived well, and they could rise through the ranks to become more powerful.

Comprising the Mongol Nation

It was into this uncertain and conflict-ridden world that the boy Temuchin was born. The Mongol nation he would build comprised over nineteen tribal groups, known as "Borjigine Kinsmen," all descended from a common ancestor called "Bodonchar the Borjigy." These tribes, which included the Adargin, Arulat, Barulas, Ba'arin, Barin, Buda'ut, Besut, Geniges, Jadarat, Jaoret, Jurkin, Kabturkhas, Khngkhotat, Mangkhut, Noyakin, Onggirat, Oronar, Sunit, Tayichi'ut, and Uru'ut, existed in a kind of confederation by the mid-1100s, and Temuchin's father, Yisugei, was a minor ruler within this confederation.

Until the thirteenth century, when the nomadic tribes unified under the leadership of Genghis Khan, they had never achieved any lasting political structure because they spent their time and energy competing among themselves. Mongol history is said to begin with Genghis Khan, for prior to his ascendancy, the Mongols were not a nation and had no written language or official records of any kind. Historians rely on archaeology and the records of other people, particularly the Chinese, to understand the history of the steppe tribes before the thirteenth century. The first written account left by the Mongol people was *The Secret History of the Mongols,* a thirteenth-century manuscript that recorded the Mongols' origins and deeds. *The Secret History* was commissioned upon the death of Genghis Khan to record the rise of the Mongol people and their conqueror's accomplishments, and it tells the story of the rise of a young man named Temuchin who would later be known as Genghis Khan.

Chapter

2 Out of Nowhere: The Rise of the Mongols

They were at Delihun Boldakh, along the Onon, and right there was Genghis Khan born; and at his birth, in his right hand, there was a clot of blood.

The Secret History of the Mongols

The Secret History of the Mongols records that Temuchin, the future conqueror who would become known to the world as Genghis Khan, was born clutching a blood clot the size of a knucklebone in his right hand. The shaman later interpreted this to be a promising sign that he would become a great warrior. Other official accounts of Temuchin's birth claim that a ray of light came through his mother's tent and announced to her "Conceive and you will bear a son who will be a world conqueror." A magical belief in the ability to conceive by a light ray was widespread among the nomads of the steppe, because Mongol shamanism considered light a powerful spirit. Historians believe Temuchin was born around A.D. 1167, although even he may never have known the exact year of his birth. Because they had no written language, the tribes of the steppe did not record dates and could not determine ages with any certainty. The Chinese traveler Zhao Hong reported in his travelogue that he often questioned Mongols about their

age, at which they would laugh and reply, "We have never known it."

The Origins of Temuchin

Temuchin's name derived from the root *temur*, meaning iron. Because he came from a family of blacksmiths, Temuchin's cradle was made of iron, and two of his siblings, Temuge and Temulun, also had names that came from the root *temur*. Temuchin's father, Yisugei, was from the Kiyat-Borjigid tribe, who were related to the Taiji'ut, a forest tribe of hunters and fishers. Yisugei had gathered a following of *nokhod* and settled by the Onon River. He was an aristocrat of the steppes, a leader, or *ba'atur*, who had proven himself adept in combat and thievery. Temuchin's mother, Ho'elun, was from the Merkit tribe. Yisugei encountered her out on the steppe while he was on a hawking expedition, and he stole her from another man who was bringing her home as a bride. Nomad men often abducted women they encountered by chance on the steppe. This was a way of avoiding the long trips normally associated with finding a wife for Mongols, who were exogamous, marrying only those outside their tribe.

A modern Mongol boy stands beside a horse, perhaps similar to one ridden by Temuchin during his childhood.

Temuchin had many siblings: an older sister, Temulun, and three brothers, Jochi-Kasar, Kachun, and Temuge, as well as two half-brothers, Bekhter and Belgutei, who were the children of his father's second wife.

Growing Up on the Steppe

In their camp by the Onon River in north-eastern Mongolia, Temuchin and his siblings learned the ways of their people. Like all Mongol children, they learned to ride horseback at an early age, and they practiced their archery by shooting at birds. In winter, they played on the ice of the Onon. Temuchin's best companion was another boy from the Jadarat tribe named Jamuka. Temuchin and Jamuka became blood brothers through a process known as the *anda*, in which they exchanged animal knucklebones for keepsakes and swore

eternal friendship. Among the nomads, the *anda* was an important pact under-taken between members of different clans, and the loyalty between sworn brothers was greater than even a blood bond. The *anda* was often affirmed by drinking from a container in which a few drops of blood from the two individuals had been mixed. Gifts such as clothing or horses were also exchanged between sworn brothers. To cement their alliance, Temuchin gave Jamuka an arrow whose head he had carved from cypress wood, and Jamuka gave Temuchin an arrow made from a calf's horn pierced with holes so that it whistled as it flew.

When Temuchin was about nine years old, his father began to look for a fiancée for his son. Mongols married at an early age and used marriage as a means of forming alliances and increasing family prestige. Yisugei sought a match for Temuchin among the Onggirat. It was a widespread custom among the Mongol nomads to send a son to live with his future parents-in-law for a year before he was married. The family of the bride insisted on this as a way to justify paying the dowry (the bride price) that came with the hand of their daughter. Yisugei chose a girl named Borte, who was a year older than Temuchin and who had the expensive dowry of a sable cloak. Thus, Yisugei left Temuchin among Borte's clan with the understanding that he would remain there for a year.

The Death of Yisugei

Riding home after leaving his son, Yisugei saw some Tartars who were feasting on the steppe. Since it was customary for nomads to offer hospitality to strangers on the steppe, Yisugei stopped at their encampment. But the Tartars recognized him as an enemy who had previously robbed them, and they secretly mixed poison in with the food they offered him. When Yisugei traveled on, he became very sick and realized he would soon die. Yisugei wanted his son to be home with his family in the event of his death, and upon reaching his camp, he sent one of his *nokhod* to summon Temuchin home. Temuchin was returned to the family camp, but after the death of Yisugei, the leaderless *nokhod* disbanded, leaving Temuchin and his family alone.

Although Ho'elun mounted a horse and carried the tribal banner in an attempt to rally the camp together again, another tribe, the Tayichi'ut, convinced Yisugei's followers to desert and join them. But the Tayichi'ut refused to accept Ho'elun and her children. And Yisugei's brothers, on whom the responsibility for Ho'elun and

her sons was supposed to fall, either refused to support her, or else she refused marriage with any one of them. As a result Ho'elun, mother of the future Genghis Khan, was left without camp, clan, or husband.

Without a tribe for support, life on the steppe was uncertain. Mongol historian Paul Ratchnevsky writes, "Nomads who separated from their tribe and lived in isolation were prey to many dangers, especially the loss of their horses, the nomads' irreplaceable possession."[8] And, indeed it was not long before Temuchin's family had its horses stolen.

Without clan or kinsmen to support them, Ho'elun and her sons lived a hand-to-mouth existence, gathering berries, hunting marmots and steppe rats, and fishing by the Onon River to feed themselves. Soon Ho'elun's sons began to complain that their half-brothers, Bekhter and Belgutei, were stealing food from them. "We caught a splendid sokosun fish," they told her, "which our brothers Bekhter and Belgutei then took from us. . . . Recently they took from us a lark which we had shot with an arrow. Now they have robbed us again. How can we live together?"[9] To ensure the survival of the clan, the division of food was of central importance in the customs of the nomads. Bekhter and Belgutei refused to honor this tradition. Ho'elun tried to convince the boys to get along, telling them that it was their responsibility to seek revenge for their humiliation by the Tayichi'ut.

Fratricide

At age fourteen, Temuchin was determined to become the head of the family.

A yurt stands isolated on the Mongolian steppe. During Temuchin's lifetime, a family without a tribe for support fell prey to hardship and robbery.

Together with his brother Jochi-Kasar, Temuchin approached Bekhter while he was out tending the horses. The two boys shot Bekhter with their arrows at close range. Bekhter made no attempt to escape or to save himself, but begged them to spare the life of his younger brother Belgutei. When Ho'elun learned of Bekhter's murder, she screamed in horror and called her sons murderers, lamenting,

> at the moment when you have no companion other than your shadow; at the moment when you have no whip other than your tail, at the moment when you are saying, "By whom shall we take vengence?" you do this to each other.[10]

After Bekhter's murder, the Tayichi'ut raided Ho'elun's river camp and took Temuchin captive out of fear that he might harm them in an attempt to seek revenge. Temuchin was held prisoner for several months, but he managed to escape by creating allies among the Tayichi'ut. One family who took a liking to him hid him, then gave him a horse and supplies. Waiting until the Tayichi'ut had a feast day, Temuchin took the opportunity to depart unnoticed and return to his family. Even at a young age, Temuchin had a charisma that fostered allies; he was aware that people's loyalties were not necessarily with their own tribe or clan.

When he returned to his family, the fifteen-year-old Temuchin sought his fiancée Borte, whom he had not seen since he was nine years old. He and Belgutei set off for the Onggirat camp and brought her home, along with her black sable cloak dowry. This cloak was meant to be Borte's present to her new mother-in-law, Ho'elun, but the family had other plans for this dowry.

Seeking Protection

Sable was considered the king of furs among the nomads of the steppe, and a good one could cost as much as two thousand gold bezants. Temuchin planned to present the cloak to a patron who would agree to protect the remnants of his family and help him to increase his following. Temuchin already had a small following through the allegiance of his brothers and another young man, Bo'Orchu. A member of the Arulat tribe, Bo'Orchu gave his support after Temuchin offered him half of his horses in exchange for having helped him recover them from thieves.

Although he realized the need to seek the protection of a powerful leader, Temuchin did not want to enter the service of a patron as a *nokhod* or mere follower; his ambition was to be a leader. Temuchin chose to ask for the patronage of Toghrul, leader of the Keraits and a former *anda* friend of his father. Temuchin said to him, "In earlier days you swore friendship with my father, Yisugei. Accordingly, you are as my own father and I bring you my wife's wedding gift." Toghrul was extremely pleased with the sable cloak and told Temuchin, "In return for the coat of black sables I shall collect for you your people who have separated themselves."[11]

Through his relationship with Toghrul, Temuchin increased his reputation among the steppe tribes. Because Toghrul, a man of repute, had taken Temuchin under his wing as a leader, and not just a mere *nokhod*, Temuchin gained many more followers as the news of his agreement with Toghrul spread. A man who had served under his father, Yisugei, offered his son to Temuchin as a squire or servant. Soon young Mongols were lining up to be Temuchin's followers and serve him under the tribal banner that Ho'elun had raised in her attempt to stop the clan from disbanding so many years before. Temuchin now had a wife, an alliance with a powerful protector, and a growing following.

The Merkit Attack

When the Merkits learned that Temuchin, then seventeen, had taken a wife, they decided that it was time to take revenge for the kidnapping of Ho'elun. The man whom Yisugei stole Ho'elun from was no longer alive, but as Mongol historian Paul Ratchnevsky has written, "Revenge was a family obligation, handed down from one generation to the next. Retribution for the deed of the father, Yisugei, must be exacted from Temuchin."[12] The practice of vendetta on the steppe ensured that a wrongdoing was always accounted for, even if by another generation. Temuchin's camp was raided by a band of three hundred Merkits. Knowing that they wanted his wife in reparation for the kidnapping of Ho'elun, Temuchin left Borte behind to be captured and barely escaped with his life. Had he sent her off on a horse and stood his ground against the Merkits, he would surely have been killed, and his clan would have been left without the protection of a leader. While abandoning Borte to the Merkits seems like a heartless gesture today, it was a commonplace one in a society where women, even Temuchin's own mother, were movable goods, captured in war and taken as bounty.

After his escape, Temuchin thanked the Eternal Blue Heaven for delivering him from danger, and he began to think that he was destined to succeed. In order to retrieve Borte, Temuchin sought the help of his new patron Toghrul. With Toghrul's help Temuchin raised an army against the Merkits and placed his childhood friend, Jamuka, at its command. Temuchin also mobilized a band of herdsmen, his first army, and led them into battle. These men were not trained warriors, but they were willing to fight for Temuchin in the hope that they could share in the looting of objects, animals, and women that accompanied successful attacks. The armies under the command of Jamuka and Temuchin defeated the Merkits, causing them to flee in the night. When the battle was over, Temuchin was reunited with Borte and triumphantly exclaimed, "I have found my necessity which I sought."[13] Shortly after Borte was rescued, she gave birth to a son they named Jochi, which means "the unexpected."

Temuchin Develops Lifelong Friendships

The Secret History of the Mongols gives this story from Temuchin's early life, as retold by Paul Ratchnevsky in Genghis Khan: His Life and Legacy:

"In broad daylight robbers (Jurkin warriors) appeared at Ho'elun's camp and in full sight of the family stole the eight geldings which were tethered in front of the tent. The family owned only one other horse, on which Belgutei had ridden out to hunt marmots. When he returned home in the evening Belgutei wanted to go in search of the stolen horses. Kasar also offered to do so but Temuchin rejected these offers. He was the eldest and, although no daredevil, would do his duty. He mounted Belgutei's horse and followed the tracks of the stolen horses. On the way he met young Bo'Orchu, the thirteen-year old son of Nayan the Rich, a member of the Arulat tribe which had maintained friendly relations with Yisugei. When Bo'Orchu discovered the purpose of Temuchin's journey he 'simply threw his leather milk bucket and ladle down on the steppe' and joined Temuchin. They found the geldings and thanks to darkness, evaded the pursuing enemy. Temuchin sought to reward Bo'Orchu for his assistance: 'Friend, would I ever have found my horses without you? Let us share them. How many do you wish?' he asks. But Bo'Orchu rejects this offer: 'I joined you because I saw that you were in trouble and in need of help. Shall I now take a share as if this were booty? What sort of service would I have rendered you? I require nothing!' This sealed a lifelong friendship between Genghis and Bo'Orchu, who. . . was one of Genghis's main supporters in the struggle for the leadership of the tribes."

Rivalry

After their victory over the Merkits, Jamuka and Temuchin traveled and camped together for over a year, although nomad groups normally separated after such campaigns. Temuchin and Jamuka were inseparable. They renewed their *anda* compact and exchanged horses and clothing that they had looted. Their camps traveled together from one grazing ground to the next. The blood brothers feasted and danced with each other, and at night they slept together under one blanket, apart from the others.

Temuchin, enriched with Merkit booty, became a serious candidate in the fight to master all the Mongol tribes. But Jamuka also wanted to lead the Mongol tribes. Despite their close friendship, there were differences between the two men. Jamuka had the support of the common men, most of whom maintained herds of sheep and had only a few horses. In contrast, Temuchin was of noble birth, and he courted the aristocracy—most of whom owned herds of horses—believing they held the key to power and prestige. These differences caused friction between the friends and eventually led Temuchin to part ways with Jamuka. Their combined camp broke up, some choosing to follow Temuchin, others staying with Jamuka.

Temuchin's magnetism and generosity, however, persuaded even some of Jamuka's followers to consider switching allegiance. Temuchin was shrewd and knew how to negotiate. To gain their loyalty, he promised them leadership positions and beautiful women if he were to become the leader of the Mongols.

Temuchin's prowess as a warrior, coupled with his nobility and generosity, made him a serious contender to lead the Mongol tribes.

People began to spread tales about Temuchin, claiming that he had a mission from heaven and that it was his destiny to become lord of the steppe. Some claimed to have witnessed a sign, in which white ox bellowed "Heaven and Earth have agreed that Temuchin shall be Lord of the Empire. I bring him this Empire." The Mongol shaman Teb-Tengri announced that the supreme deity, the Eternal Blue Heaven, had also told him "I have given the whole surface of the earth to Temuchin and to his sons."[14] Temuchin himself believed he had a mandate from heaven, announcing "My strength was fortified by Heaven and Earth. Foreordained [for this] by Mighty Heaven, I was brought here by Mother Earth."[15]

A Reputation for Generosity

Because Temuchin had no tribe of his own, he had to recruit followers, or *nokhod*, by earning a reputation as a fair and generous leader. Temuchin was generous to those who joined him, giving them horses and furs. Many who were suffering under unkind leaders switched their allegiance to him, saying, "The Prince [Temuchin] dresses his people in his own clothes, he permits them to ride his own horses; this man could certainly bring peace to the tribe and rule the nation."[16] Temuchin's reputation grew, and individuals as well as groups from many different tribes wanted to become his *nokhod*. Mongol people of various clans saw him as their champion, the one who would unite all the Mongol tribes.

Meanwhile, the Mongol chieftains who had chosen to side with Temuchin over Jamuka had begun to agree that they needed a single person to lead them, although none of them trusted or was willing to serve under any of the others. But Temuchin, whose prowess and persona were quickly becoming legendary, was seen as a fair and trustworthy leader. In addition, Temuchin's father had been a chieftain, and this aristocratic background marked him as a man of good lineage. So in 1183, the Mongol chieftains held a meeting and elected Temuchin as their khan, or ruler. The chieftains promised that Temuchin should ride at the head of their people, always leading them against their enemies, and that they would throw

As Temuchin's reputation grew, so grew the numbers of his nokhod, *or followers. In 1183 the ambitious warrior was elected khan by some of the steppe tribes, a position through which many people hoped he would be able to unite the fractured Mongol horde.*

themselves "like lightning" upon his foes. They promised to obey him in war and not to interfere in his affairs in times of peace. *The Secret History* records the oath made to Temuchin before his election as khan:

> When you are khan, Temuchin, we will ride as your spearhead against the multitudinous enemy and bring back their beautiful women and maidens and their ceremonial tents; and from the foreign tribes we will bring comely women and maidens, also their fine-limbed geldings at a trot, and present them to you. When we hunt the wild animals, we will be in the van [forefront] of the hunters and will give you

[the slaughtered animals]. We will drive the steppe animals towards you in such numbers that their rumps touch. If, on the day of battle, we do not obey your commands, separate us from our belongings, from our wives and our women and throw our black heads away on the empty steppe. If, in time of peace, we break our word to you, separate us from our servants, from our women and children and banish us to a leaderless land.[17]

Uniting the Tribes

Temuchin's election as khan in 1183 did not make him leader of all the Mongols. The majority of the Mongol tribes, and the most powerful among them, such as the Tayichi'ut, the Onggirat, and the Arulat, supported Jamuka. But Temuchin, then about thirty-four years old, was bent on using the power of his new title to further his own dream of ruling over all the Mongol people. Although Temuchin was leader of only a few tribes of Mongols, he took his new position very seriously and began to organize his followers in unprecedented ways.

Previously, the Mongols had lacked any social organization. But Temuchin divided his followers into groups that had specific duties to the community. He placed some men in charge of providing food and drink for his army, while others were made messengers, horse trainers, herdsmen, swordsmen, archers, or were put in charge of managing the slaves and servants or maintaining the tent wagons. He chose a commanding officer for each camp, and those followers who had been beside him from the beginning were rewarded with these high positions. He also appointed a number of loyal youths as his bodyguards, armed with bows and arrows. Temuchin made it a practice to flatter and reward loyal supporters, but he treated those who broke his trust with utter cruelty.

Fighting Jamuka

Toghrul was pleased that one of his vassals had been elected khan, but Jamuka was angry. Soon after Temuchin's election, one of Jamuka's tribesmen stole some horses that belonged to a Jalair tribesman who had become one of Temuchin's people. The Jalair man launched a revenge attack and killed one of Jamuka's followers. This incident provided the pretext for Jamuka to declare war on Temuchin.

Thirty thousand warriors drawn from fourteen tribes attacked Temuchin, who met the attack with a smaller force of thirteen camps. Jamuka's forces defeated Temuchin's, and the new khan was forced to seek refuge in the narrow Jerene Pass near the upper part of the Onon River. Jamuka allowed Temuchin to escape, but he murdered most of Temuchin's followers who had been taken prisoner. The remaining captives were boiled to death in seventy large cauldrons, a common method of execution that was believed to prevent a victim's spirit from surviving and taking revenge from beyond the grave. Jamuka also tied the heads of two of Temuchin's murdered chieftains to his horse's tail.

After his defeat Temuchin was forced to leave the Onon valley and resettle farther south, near Toghrul, in the valley of the river Kerulen. Here, despite his humiliating defeat, Temuchin continued to gather followers. Temuchin was undeterred from his goal of ruling the steppe, but he was not yet powerful enough to conquer his enemies. During this time, however, a series of four wars reversed his fortunes.

Shifting Alliances

Around 1198 when the northern Chinese were raided by tribes of Tartars, they launched a military expedition that forced the Tartar chief to retreat into Mongolia's Ulja valley. Toghrul and Temuchin, eager for an alliance with the Chinese, sought this opportunity to massacre the defeated Tartar horde. In return, the Chinese gave Temuchin and Toghrul special advantages in the frontier trade for Chinese goods. This special consideration from the Chinese made it appear as if Temuchin and Toghrul were in league with the Chinese. The imagined partnership caused fear in the other tribal groups and they rallied around Jamuka for protection.

As a result, Jamuka attracted many followers and Temuchin no longer had the majority of supporters. In 1201 the chiefs of all the eastern tribal groups, headed by Jamuka, whom they had declared their khan, battled Temuchin and Toghrul's forces. Jamuka was defeated but managed to escape. Among those Temuchin defeated were the Tajik and the remaining Tartar groups, whose survivors were absorbed into his own conglomerate army. This caused those tribes to cease to exist as identifiable entities. Temuchin often completed his conquests by absorbing the vanquished into the Mongol horde.

Although Toghrul and Temuchin's alliance had resulted in victory for both of them, it made Toghrul's son, Sanghum, uneasy. Fearing the power that Temuchin had accumulated, Sanghum began to consider Temuchin a threat to his own future. He managed to convince his father that something had to be done to curb Temuchin's rising power. In 1203 the powerful alliance collapsed, and Toghrul and his son turned on Temuchin. They attacked Temuchin's camp. Temuchin was caught off guard, and his forces were routed. Temuchin himself barely escaped the battlefield into the night. Regrouping, he and his men later in the same year made a surprise attack on Toghrul's camp. Victorious, Temuchin rose from battle to become the ruler of the people he had vanquished in battle.

The Naimans

Temuchin knew there was one more war to fight before he could consolidate all of the steppe tribes. Some fugitives from the defeated tribes had joined forces with the last significant power to oppose Temuchin: the Naiman tribe. The Naimans, who were of Turkic origin and practiced Buddhism, were longtime enemies of the Mongol tribes. Jamuka, in a last-ditch attempt to defeat Temuchin, had allied with the Naiman king, and the two were plotting Temuchin's downfall. Neither side felt confident enough to make a hasty move, and thus both bided their time for about a year, collecting and organizing their forces. To prepare himself for the eventual confrontation with the Naiman armies, Temuchin called a meeting of all the tribal leaders under his command and took the time to restructure his armies.

A Mongol warrior prepares for battle in this mural from the Shalu Monastery in Tibet. With Temuchin's able guidance, Mongol soldiers were molded into a highly efficient, cohesive army.

Temuchin divided his mounted cavalry into groups of tens, hundreds, and thousands. Each squad consisted of ten mounted warriors, and there were ten squads in a squadron and 10 squadrons in a *quran* of one thousand men. Ten *qurans* formed a *tuman* of ten thousand riders. The light cavalry carried missile weapons while the heavy cavalry was equipped for hand-to-hand combat. Daily drills and practice runs taught the men how to respond to commands and move as units. The best warriors led the *qurans*, and they were perfectly obedient to Temuchin.

The nomads of the steppe traditionally fought defensively, from within a circle of wagons. But Temuchin devised a new fighting strategy: The light cavalry was arranged in front of heavily armed foot soldiers positioned in a long line. Behind them the heavy cavalry waited to exploit weaknesses in an enemy line or to harass an enemy in retreat. The *qurans*, or groups of one thousand, were arranged in a block that was one-hundred-men wide and ten-men deep. As the enemy advanced, the mounted soldiers were to ride ahead, shoot a storm of arrows, then fall back as the foot soldiers advanced. These infantry units were well armed and carried heavy axes and scimitars. After the light cavalry disrupted the enemy, the foot soldiers and heavy cavalry would, with luck, overwhelm the disorganized enemy. Only the women and children were to remain far off to one side, barricaded within the circle of tent wagons.

The Battle Begins

After unfurling his battle colors on the day of the Feast of the Moon in 1204, the year of the rat, Temuchin marched with his armies to the neighboring Naiman territory. By the time they neared the enemy's camp, the Mongol horses were exhausted, and Temuchin's scouts reported that the Naiman army was a force of greatly superior numbers. Temuchin decided to make camp and rest the horses. According to a plan devised by one of his commanders, Temuchin ordered that hundreds more campfires than necessary be lit, a move which fooled the Naimans into believing that they were up against a much larger army.

When the two forces finally joined in battle, Jamuka noted the improved tactics of Temuchin's formations and quickly left

This painting from a Persian manuscript portrays Mongol warfare, including the use of heavily armed foot soldiers and mounted cavalry.

the battlefield. Jamuka feared the newly organized army, and he was also uncertain whether he could trust his people to fight with the Naimans, the traditional enemy of their people, against other Mongols. Disheartened by the desertion of their ally, the Naiman army collapsed under the weight of Temuchin's forces. The Naiman king died of wounds received in the battle, and his son fled to evade capture. According to *The Secret History*, "Thus, in the foothills of the Altai, Genghis Khan put an end to the Naiman nation and made it his own."[18]

Following his flight from battle, Jamuka hid himself in exile, but he was eventually captured by the Mongols. Although Temuchin always treated his rivals mercilessly, Jamuka was his childhood companion and *anda*. To kill an *anda* was more terrible than fratricide in Mongol culture. In their final discussion, Temuchin begged Jamuka to be his friend once again. Ja-

muka felt this to be impossible: "When I should have been a good companion, I was no companion to you. Now, my friend, you have pacified the peoples of this region and have united alien lands. The supreme throne is yours."[19] According to legend, Jamuka then requested to be executed.

Changing the Balance of Power

The wars between Temuchin and his opponents completely reorganized the power structure on the steppe. With the removal of all significant opposition through battle and the absorption of tribes, the tribal states of the steppes now became organized under a single supreme government controlled by Temuchin, the leader of the Mongols. This unification of the steppe tribes had far-reaching consequences.

Chapter

3 Building a Nation

In 1206 a meeting of chiefs, known as the *quriltai*, was held, and Temuchin, then about thirty-nine years old—past his prime by medieval standards—was declared the absolute master of all the tribes of Mongolia. He was enthroned as the Great Khan of the Mongolian nation, which was a single entity for the first time, stretching from the Altai Mountains in the west to the Khingan Mountains in the east, and from Lake Baikal to the Gobi Desert. He received the new title of Genghis Khan, meaning "Oceanic ruler," which signified supreme power and strength.

Temuchin, now Genghis Khan, had consolidated all of the tribes, and hence all of the military power north of the Gobi Desert, and now made it his mission to harness this power effectively. By emphasizing each warrior's loyalty to the army, and making himself the focus of the army's loyalty, Genghis created a superior military machine that was responsive to his whims. Similarly, Genghis attempted to forge a government which, like the *nokhod* system, favored loyalty and allegiance over lineage.

The steppe tribes shared similar nomadic customs, but until Genghis Khan set out to create one, they had no state. As self-governing nomadic people, the tribes' customs had always sufficed to organize them, and they had never had a need for

an administration. Because they had no central government, civil offices, written language, or places to train civil servants, the Mongols started building their state from the bottom up. As with his army, Genghis believed organization and loyalty would be the key to the success of the Mongol state.

Rewarding Loyal Followers

His first act upon ascending the throne was to reward the loyal followers whose steadfastness and sacrifice had enabled him to achieve victory. *The Secret History* devotes twenty-one paragraphs to describing the services rendered to Genghis Khan by his supporters and the rewards that Genghis Khan subsequently bestowed upon them. Genghis chose from among his most loyal followers when he set up the command structure of his army. To Bo'Orchu, who as a young man had helped Temuchin retrieve his stolen horses without expecting anything in return, he bestowed a commanding military position. Remarkable among rulers of his time, Genghis did not choose family members for key positions. He was somewhat skeptical about family allegiance and hesitant to install relatives for

A generous leader, Genghis Khan (seated on throne) rewarded loyal followers with positions in his military.

fear they might betray him, but Genghis was generous and trusting toward those who were not his relatives but who had proved their loyalty to him in battle.

Creating a Power Structure

Experience had taught Genghis that he could not trust the individual clans, or his relatives, or even an *anda* mate. He had managed to emerge from an extremely marginal position on the steppe to one of great power and influence, but he realized that support was fickle and loyalties were easily shifted. To maintain control over an army of approximately one hundred thousand men required loyalty.

To ensure that his soldiers' loyalty was to Genghis and the nation and not to their tribe, he tried to weaken the power of the individual tribes. And he promoted men based on their leadership and skill rather than their social status or family background.

To weaken tribal unity as well as the power of the tribal leaders, Genghis created military units that were not based on tribal loyalties. He mixed men from many tribes and put them in the same unit, under the control of a man who was from yet another tribe.

Genghis also recognized those with superior skills, regardless of their class or race, and ensured that they were promoted. His army was a meritocracy, and shepherds or stable boys could command regiments if they proved worthy. In many cases, this meant that aristocrats became subject to the orders of commoners who had been appointed to leadership positions on the basis of their achievements. The entire nation became divided into military, rather than tribal, units. This military reorganization differed dramatically from the tradition of organizing armies along tribal lines, and

The Strength of the Empire

To ensure that the empire he founded would last after his death, Genghis sought to create harmony between his sons, convincing them that they must work together for their own good. In Volume 1 of The History of the World Conqueror, *translated by J. A. Boyle, Ata-Malik Juvaini recorded this image of Genghis gathering his children and illustrating the power of unity under one khan.*

"One day he called his sons together and taking an arrow from his quiver he broke it in half. Then he took two arrows and broke them also. And he continued to add to the bundle until there were so many arrows that even athletes were unable to break them. Then turning to his sons he said: 'So it is with you also. A frail arrow, when it is multiplied and supported by its fellows, not even mighty warriors are able to break it but in impotence withdraw their hands therefrom. As long, therefore, as you brothers support one another and render stout assistance one to another, though your enemies be men of great strength and might, yet shall they not gain the victory over you. But if there be no leader among you, to whose counsel the other brothers, and sons, and helpmeets [helpmates], and companions submit themselves and to whose command they yield obedience, then your case will be like unto that of the snake of many heads. One night, when it was bitterly cold, the heads desired to creep into a hole in order to ward off the chill. But as each head entered the hole another head would oppose it; and in this way they all perished. But another snake, which had but one head and a long tail, entered the hole and found room for his tail and all his limbs and members, which were preserved from the fury of the cold."

it subsequently changed the social structure of the Mongol nation.

Chain of Command

The leaders of the *qurans* (units of one thousand) were the principal operating officers of the Mongol army; in 1206, there were ninety-five of them. These men were governed in turn by the officers of *tumans*. The reorganization of the Mongol army gave them complete superiority over the armies of even the most powerful and civilized states of that time. The Mongol army quickly developed a reputation for invincibility. According to Friar Giovanni of Plano Carpini, who traveled among the Mongols in the 1240s,

> [Genghis] Khan ordained that the army should be organised in such a way that over ten men should be set one man and he is what we call a captain of ten; over ten of these should be placed one, named a captain of a hundred; at the head of ten captains of a hundred is placed a soldier known as a captain of a thousand, and over ten captains of a thousand is one man, and the word they use for this number means "darkness." Two or three chiefs are in command of the whole army, yet in such a way that one holds the supreme command.[20]

To fill his army, Genghis Khan introduced a policy of conscription for all males aged fifteen to seventy. Doctors, priests, and undertakers were exempt from military duty, and men from conquered nations were subject to different conscription rules because their loyalty to the Mongol nation could not be ensured.

Under punishment of death, men were not allowed to leave the units to which they had been assigned. Likewise, their families, who traveled with them and were responsible for providing their mili-

Allegiance to the Military

Friar Giovanni of Plano Carpini's description of Mongol loyalty has been translated in Mission to Asia, *a collection of travel accounts edited by Christopher Dawson.*

"When they are going in battle, if one or two or three or even more out of a group of ten run away, all are put to death; and if a whole group of ten flees, the rest of the group of a hundred are put to death, if they do not flee too. In a word, unless they retreat in a body, all who take flight are put to death. Likewise, if one or two or more go forward boldly to the fight, then the rest of the ten are put to death if they do not follow and, if one or more of the ten are captured, their companions are put to death if they do not rescue them."

tary equipment, were also subject to the control of the unit commander. The new military nobility created by this power structure owed their status to the ruler, so they were completely loyal to him.

The Apparatus of War

When new arrivals reached the military camp, or *ordu*, they found it laid out along a standard pattern, so that the medical tent, the armory, and so forth, were always in the same locations. The *ordus* were run by quartermasters known as *jurtchis*, who were responsible for allocating and organizing supplies. Weapons and other equipment were distributed to the men, but each soldier was responsible for making sure his equipment was kept in good shape. A Mongol warrior's equipment began with his clothing, which was designed to protect him. Each warrior wore a tightly woven silk undershirt, an innovation learned from the Chinese. The silk shirt helped the warrior if an arrow pierced his armor, for the arrow would not pierce the woven silk but would drag it into the wound. This enabled the physician or soldier to remove the arrowhead by gently pulling on the silk around the wound. Otherwise, removing an arrowhead embedded in flesh meant creating a much larger wound than that created by the arrow.

Over this silk undershirt each warrior wore a tunic, and if he were part of the heavy cavalry that would engage in hand-to-hand combat, he would also wear a coat of chain mail armor and a breastplate made of leather studded with strip metal. To protect his calves, warrior's boots had squares of iron sewn into the lining. In addition, each warrior carried a leather-covered, lightweight wicker shield, and those of high rank wore a helmet of leather or iron.

Standard weaponry included two composite bows and a large quiver of at least sixty arrows. Light cavalry carried a small sword and two or three javelins, while the heavy cavalry were armed with a scimitar, a battle axe or mace, and a twelve-foot lance.

On his horse, each soldier carried clothing, cooking pots, dried meat, a water bottle, files for sharpening arrows, and a needle and thread. The saddlebag that held some of these items was also useful, as it was made from a cow's stomach and was waterproof and inflatable. If necessary, it could be used as a flotation device when crossing rivers.

Readiness for War

Every man had to be ready for war at a moment's notice. Upon being called for service, the men would be expected to travel, along with four or five horses, to wherever their unit was based. With extra mounts for each warrior, the Mongol army was able to advance for days at a time with remarkable speed. A man's wife was responsible for keeping his saddlebags constantly filled with dried meat and milk curds, and his leather pouch filled with *koumiss*, so he would be ready at short notice for a journey. She also had to make sure his sheepskin cloak, felt socks, and leather boots were ready for wear.

Unlike many of their thirteenth-century counterparts, Mongol women were in charge of all of their husbands' possessions, and they could trade, buy, and sell according to their judgment. A Mongol

Genghis Khan (top) and a companion are depicted during a falcon hunt in this Chinese silk painting. To prepare his army for war, Genghis incorporated the tactics used in hunting into specialized war games.

woman's primary responsibility, however, was to increase the reputation of her husband, thereby helping him to become a more respected individual. If the army was going far, wives and children would follow the armies at a distance. If the army was traveling abroad, the family herds would also be brought to provide food over a long period of time. The nomadic lives of the Mongols helped to make them especially suited to extended military campaigns, as they were able to bring all the trappings of home, making their lives on the march more comfortable.

War Games

To drill his army, Genghis Khan incorporated the nomads' love of hunting into military exercises. While hunting for deer, wild boar, and wolf, the warriors learned to think and act as one unit. Every winter for three months, hunting exercises, or war games, were conducted, and every man was required to participate in these team hunts. The same techniques used to kill game would later be employed on the battlefield.

One such tactic was known as the "feint," in which the prey was goaded into attacking one or two horsemen, who would then gallop away, drawing the animal into a trap. Once the prey was in the intended place, a circle of waiting horsemen would move in for the kill. The feint tactic was adapted to the battlefield through a corps of horsemen, called the "suicide troops," or *mangudai*, who would work to bring the enemy to the place where a larger force of Mongol troops lay in wait. The *mangudai* would charge straight at the enemy line, then, approaching firing range, turn suddenly and retreat at a gallop. Enemy commanders usually followed suit, and soon the *mangudai* would lead the enemy into the prepared ambush.

The Mongols had many such methods of improving their combat skills while on the hunt. One of their most fantastic maneuvers was a "circle and close-in" tactic described here by author Robert Marshall:

Another approach was to string an entire division of the army along what

---

Genghis Khan's Religious Tolerance

In The History of the World Conqueror, *Persian historian Ata-Malik Juvaini recorded Genghis's respect for all religions. However, like many of his contemporaries, Juvaini failed to recognize that Genghis practiced shamanism, and took the erroneous view that the Mongols had no religion at all.*

"Being the adherent of no religion and the follower of no creed, [Genghis Khan] eschewed bigotry, and the preference of one faith to another, and the placing of some above others; rather he honoured and respected the learned and pious of every sect, recognizing such conduct as the way to the Court of God. And as he viewed the Moslems with the eye of respect, so also did he hold the Christians and idolaters in high esteem. As for his children and grandchildren, several of them have chosen a religion according to their inclination, some adopting Islam, others embracing Christianity, others selecting idolatry and others again cleaving to the ancient canon of their fathers and forefathers and inclining in no direction; but these are now a minority. But though they have adopted some religion they still for the most part avoid all show of fanaticism and do not swerve from the yasa of [Genghis Khan], namely, to consider all sects as one and not to distinguish them from one another."

might be described as a starting line, sometimes 130 km (80 miles) long. On a signal the entire complement, fully armed as if for battle, would ride forward at a walk towards a finish line hundreds of miles away. This was usually situated at a point in the shadow of a hill, where the proceedings could be watched by the khan and his entourage. Over the following days the massed cavalry would march forward, sweeping or herding before them all the game they encountered along the way. . . . During the hunt, as the riders approached the finish line the flanks would begin to ride ahead of the center, and so slowly describe a massive arc. Still further on, the flanks would turn and ride towards each other, thus trapping all the game that had been herded over the hundreds of kilometers of countryside. During the march it was forbidden to kill anything, but it was even more of a disgrace if a rider let some beast escape the net. Throughout the exercise officers rode behind their men, shouting orders and directing their movements.[21]

At the end of this exercise, the khan would ride down from his vantage point and take his pick of game from the tightened circle, an act that would put his own hunting skills on display before the entire unit. Once the khan had done this, each individual soldier had a chance to show off his skills with sword, lance, or bow in front of his officers. Hunting skills like these were easily transformed into battle skills. By performing the same operation against the enemy, enemy troops could be surrounded without realizing it.

A Communication Revolution

To coordinate the maneuvers of the commanders and their troops, Genghis needed an effective system of communication that could bridge the distance created by Mongolia's 380 million acres of steppe land.

To keep informed of what was happening in even the farthest reaches of the empire, the Mongols created an elaborate communications network, known as the *Yam*, that was state-of-the-art for the thirteenth century. The system relied on flag or torch signals, as well as riders, to relay messages. These riders were official envoys of the khan, and they often rode without stopping day or night, even sleeping in the saddle. Imperial riders wore bells that signaled their approach to way stations, where a fresh horse would be waiting in the road. When they needed a fresh mount, the nearest horse, no matter who it belonged to, had to be handed over by order of the khan. Often the messengers did not dismount but changed horses at a full gallop. In this way, the imperial messengers could cover a distance that normally took weeks in only a few days.

In times of war, these riders traveled great distances to deliver information from one commander to another, as the battlefronts were often very broad. As a result all of the units could be in contact. This enabled the khan to control his vast army on many different fronts. It also gave the Mongols a distinct advantage over their enemies, who had difficulty coordinating their large armies.

Battle Tactics

Genghis Khan's troops were so well drilled that they could respond to commands instantly as a coordinated unit. Genghis always wanted his soldiers to take the initiative in battle, so his warriors always attacked, even when they were defending territory. The discipline of the Mongol troops, combined with their superior battlefield tactics, always succeeded in vanquishing the enemy.

Genghis loved to use the element of surprise in battle, and he seldom repeated patterns of movement in the same campaign, which made it difficult for the enemy to apprehend his tactics. Sometimes the soldiers would pretend to retreat, but once out of the way, they would mount fresh horses and attack, outrunning the enemy's tired mounts. Often the light cavalry would distract the enemy on the front while other Mongol units closed in from all sides to overpower the enemy.

The *Keshig*

Another feature that made the Mongol army so formidable was the core unit of unconditionally loyal followers who would carry out the khan's policies, whatever they may be. Genghis used this unit as his personal corps of bodyguards, or *keshig*. Although originally a group of seventy day guards and eighty night guards, by the time of his election as khan in 1206, the *keshig* had expanded to a force of ten thousand. They were responsible for protecting the khan as well as handpicking messengers and warriors for special missions. The

This Chinese illustration depicts the Mongol warrior and statesman Genghis Khan carrying a bow and quiver. Genghis's capable leadership and tactical genius made the Mongol army nearly invincible.

keshig were granted special privileges and enjoyed a rank above that of even the military commanders. Some of the men chosen for this elite group were the brothers and sons of the military commanders. They functioned as hostages, for if any one of the military commanders were to disobey Genghis, punishment for his misdeeds could be brought to bear on his brother or son in the bodyguard corps. Thus Genghis felt secure that he could exact the loyalty of both his commanders and his *keshig*. Because the *keshig* proved to be an unconditionally loyal cadre of troops, administrators for the empire were later chosen from among them.

In addition to revolutionizing the military, Genghis Khan made important changes in the Mongol social system. These changes were designed to bring peace and order to the society as well as to the individual families and clans.

Establishing a Code of Law

Soon after his election as khan, Genghis established a legal code known as the "Yasa." The Yasa, which grew to contain a body of case histories—accounts of judicial decisions that could serve as legal precedents—began as a list of laws handed down by Genghis. This code of laws became the institutional foundation for the Mongol Empire, and it contained Genghis's wisdom and vision for the future. He wanted all the decrees, directives, and orders for the administration of the empire set in writing, and he chose to adopt the Uighur script, which had been used by the Naimans, and adapt it to the Mongolian language. By writing down the laws and teaching his administrators how to read the Uighur script, Genghis felt there would be a greater permanence to the Yasa. He issued a warning to those who deviated from the laws in the Yasa: "If the great, the military leaders, the emirs of the many descendants of the ruler who will be born in the future, should not adhere strictly to the law, then the power of the state will be shattered and come to an end."[22]

Although this collection of laws was constantly expanded, the basic principles of the Yasa were laid down in 1206. The Yasa codified some Mongol common law, such as the traditions against lying or interfering in the disagreements of others. Religious taboos were also codified. Death was the punishment for behavior that offended the Mongol gods, such as urinating in a stream or river. The theft of a nomad's animal was also punishable by death, since it robbed the victim of his ability to sustain himself. But most of the Yasa laws pertained to situations brought about by the transformation of Mongol society from a nomad state to an empire. Strict laws dedicated to military organization were laid down. On the homefront women were obliged to perform all of their husband's tasks if he were away at war. On the battlefield, if a soldier failed to pick up a bow or quiver another soldier had dropped during battle, or if he deserted or became a spy for the enemy, death was mandatory. Fines were imposed for certain behaviors, such as robbery, and the punishment for the most serious crimes was execution. Official orders recorded in Uighur script were to be legalized with the stamp of a state seal.

The administrative division of the empire into separate *ulus* (areas of territory over which to rule) eventually led to the development of individual *yasas* suited to the different social and political situations within the empire. Conscription law, for example, differed by region. The new codes of laws helped instill fear among the population, and cases of theft, murder, robbery, and adultery, which had been so numerous in Temuchin's youth, eventually decreased.

The tribes did not concede power to the khan's government easily, however. Many resented the government's interference in the traditional rights of the tribal

A Mongol warrior retrieves a fallen lance while his comrades display their horsemanship. According to Yasa law, death was a mandatory punishment for a soldier who failed to pick up a fellow warrior's weapon during battle.

chiefs. But they either feared military reprisal or were unable to organize an effective resistance to the newly organized society.

Providing for the People

Genghis had risen to power on his reputation. He was generous and kind toward his own people, and these were traits the nomads valued in a leader. Genghis still considered it his tribal obligation to see that all members of Mongol society benefited from his policies. For example, he devised a tax on the army for the purpose of providing cattle, felt, and cheese made from sheep's milk to those who could not support themselves because of injury or unfortunate circumstances. He even maintained an orphan fund for the children of soldiers who were killed in battle.

"Heaven and earth grew weary of the excessive pride in luxury in China," Genghis once explained Mongol social relations in a letter to the Taoist sage Ch'ang-Ch'un. "I am from the barbaric North. . . . I wear the same clothing and eat the same food as the cowherds and horse-herders. We make the same sacrifices and we share our riches. I look upon the nation as a newborn child and I care for my soldiers as if they were my brothers."[23] Unlike China's highly differentiated social structure, with its elaborate forms of address for leaders, Mongol society had few divisions among people. While the Chinese pronounced names differently, according to social rank, Genghis insisted that his name be pronounced the same way as everyone else's. Genghis's policies earned him respect and kept his soldiers loyal and willing to follow his orders for the well-being of themselves and their nation.

The Beginnings of Foreign Expansion

Most historians concur that once he had conquered all internal resistance, Genghis began to look outward and focus on becoming master of the steppe. The Mongols considered the sedentary territories to the east and west of them, such as parts of China and the Middle East, as only marginally important. They could provide tribute and riches, but once the Mongol armies conquered and pillaged these regions they withdrew, leaving behind only a skeleton crew to collect the tribute. The Mongols were content not to take an active role in their affairs as long as they received some of these countries' wealth.

The first expansion of Mongol territory came in 1209, when the Uighurs of western central Asia broke with the Buddhist Empire of the Quara Khitai (which was based in central Asia near the Persian border) and offered their allegiance to Genghis Khan. The Uighur state was welcomed; it provided tribute and remained au-

tonomous throughout Genghis's lifetime. The Uighurs' submission created a precedent whereby those states that willingly submitted to the Mongol Empire were allowed vassal-like autonomy. Genghis preferred to secure submission from his neighbors without resorting to warfare.

In 1209 the Mongols set their sights on the kingdom of Xixia in present-day western China, which was ruled by the Tibetan-speaking Tangut people. Xixia was renowned for its fine cloth, and it also controlled oases along the Silk Road, from which it demanded a heavy toll on traveling Mongol caravans. Some of Genghis's tribal enemies are believed to have fled to Xixia to escape his rule. Fear of organized reprisal from these enemies may also have prompted the Mongols' attack on Xixia.

After crossing the Gobi Desert to engage the kingdom's defenders, the Mongols, faced with a large enemy force, feigned retreat. As the Tanguts broke ranks and chased them, the Mongol army turned and crushed the disorganized pursuers. The Mongols captured the Tangut leader in battle, but they spared his life and allowed him to remain king as long as he agreed to send troops to the Mongols if asked. The Tangut king gave Genghis his daughter in marriage, and Xixia became a vassal state.

The Campaign Against Northern China

East of the Xixia lay the kingdom of the Jurchen, who called their dynasty "Chin," meaning "golden." The Jurchen ruled over northern China. And while they had always bribed the nomads to prevent them from attacking, by the beginning of the thirteenth century the Jurchen were undergoing political and economic problems. The native Chinese resented Jurchen rule, and disloyalty was rampant in the army. From his intelligence, which included merchants and defecting Chin civil servants, Genghis knew that the Chin regime was weak. He also knew that most of the six-hundred-thousand-man-strong Chin army

The army of Genghis Khan surrounds a Chinese fortress, preparing to storm the walls.

was embroiled in the south, where the regime battled China's Sung dynasty.

In 1211 Genghis, now approximately forty-four years old, led an army of seventy thousand into Chin territory. Many battles later, in 1214, Genghis's army surrounded the Chin capital at Shang-tu, which was fortified by forty-foot walls. Using catapults powered by plunging weights, the Mongols were ready to hurl one-hundred-pound stones against the city's walls and gates. But the Chin emperor offered the Mongols gold and silver and agreed to give Genghis a Chin princess if he withdrew his troops. The Khan agreed, but one year later, when rumors spread that the Chin were regrouping to attack the Mongols, Genghis's army took the Chin capital, mercilessly slaughtering its inhabitants. Mongol horsemen rode through the streets firing flaming arrows into the wooden houses. Whole districts were burned to the ground, and one eyewitness, an ambassador of the Khwarazm Shah, leader of the Islamic Empire in western Asia, recorded that after all the carnage and fire, the streets were greasy with human fat and covered with carcasses. The Mongols left with piles of Chin treasures, leaving behind a Mongol general to look after their interests. Years later, travelers to Shang-tu recorded that what appeared to be a white hill in the city was really a pile of bones, the remnants of Shang-tu's citizens.

Terror as a Tactic of War

The Mongol attack on the Chin was akin to genocide. The population of northern China, which had been fifty million in 1195, plummeted to only nine million by 1226. But the destruction of Shang-tu was intended as a warning to others. Hearing of the fate of the city, the Koreans immediately dispatched diplomats to the Mongols, offering to pay substantial tribute in exchange for being left alone. The submission of the Koreans proved that Genghis's terror tactic was working.

Since the Mongols did not have the manpower to station garrisons in every territory they vanquished, they relied on the fear and memories of the conquered to ensure loyalty in the absence of a military presence. The Arab chronicler Ibn al-Athir recorded, "In the countries that have not yet been overrun by them, everyone spends the night afraid that they may appear there too."[24]

According to one theory, Genghis wanted to leave no city intact to aid his enemies. Although the death toll in ravaged cities was high, the Mongols did not arbitrarily slaughter all civilians. Anyone with a unique skill—such as astronomers, blacksmiths, weavers, physicians, scribes, and falconers—were transported, along with their wives and children, to Mongolia. Genghis Khan knew that he could use their knowledge to help develop his empire. Furthermore, the lives of women, craftsmen, and others were often spared so that the Mongols would have people to help move their pack trains and siege weapons; they also could be sold or given away as slaves or used for their skill.

Cities that surrendered to the Mongols without a fight escaped such destruction. In return, they had to provide a yearly tribute and conscripts to the Mongols. Many rulers chose to yield to the Mongols rather than face them. Thus when the Mongol army sacked Baghdad in 1258, it included conscripted soldiers from Persia, Georgia, and Armenia.

Arousing Fear in Others

In Michel Hoang's Genghis Khan, *Kirakos of Ganjak, an Armenian historian captured by the Mongols and pressed into their service as a secretary, remarks on the Mongols' unkempt appearance and their course eating habits.*

"They were hideous and terrifying to look at, beardless, although some of them had a few hairs growing on their chins or their upper lips. Their eyes were narrow and keen, their voices shrill and piercing; their life was a hard one and they were intrepid. When they had the opportunity they ate constantly and drank greedily; when there was no such opportunity they were abstinent. They ate all living things, whether cleaned or not, and what they liked best was horse meat, of which they would cut off one chunk after another and boil it or roast it without salt. . . . Some of them ate kneeling, like camels, others sitting down. . . . And if someone brought them something to eat or drink they first forced the person offering it to eat or drink some of it himself, as if they were afraid they were being given some fatal poison."

The Empire of the Khwarazm Shah

Hearing about the fall of Shang-tu, the Khwarazm Shah, also known as the Shah Muhammed, was anxious to speak with Genghis Khan. The shah's Islamic Empire comprised modern-day Uzbekistan and parts of Persia, now known as Iran. The magnificent Silk Road trading cities of Bukhara and Samarkand were under his control. He was a powerful ruler and had contemplated conquering China himself until his ambassadors told him of the Mongol victory and the atrocities at Shang-tu. As soon as the news of the Mongols' conquest of the Chin reached the shah, Bukharan merchants set out to visit the Mongol realm. Genghis Khan gave them jade, gold, ivory, and cloaks made from the wool of white camels to deliver as gifts to the shah. They also brought him a letter from Genghis Khan that read:

I send you these gifts. I know your power and the vast extent of your empire and I regard you as my most cherished son. For your part you must know that I have conquered China and all the Turkish nations north of it; my country is an anthill of soldiers and a mine of silver and I have no need of other lands. Therefore I believe that we have an equal interest in encouraging trade between our subjects.[25]

Some historians believe Genghis Khan was trying to trick Khwarazm Shah into believing that he had no interest in attacking

After his envoys were killed by the Khwarazm Shah, Genghis (pictured) prepared to exact his vengeance on the disloyal shah.

his kingdom in order to give his armies time to recover from the Chin conquest and prepare to conquer the empire of the shah. Other historians doubt that Genghis, whose troops were already seriously overextended, could have been planning war against the shah at the time when he sent the letter. Meanwhile, the shah regarded the Mongols as a threat and had no intention of allowing his empire to become a Mongol vassal state. He accepted Genghis's offer of peace but secretly began preparing for war.

In 1218 a caravan of 450 Muslim merchants traveled from Mongol territory to the eastern border of the Khwarazm Shah's empire, inaugurating the trade agreement between the two emperors. But the governor of the shah's eastern territory, claiming that the merchants were spies, confiscated their merchandise and killed them all. Such an accusation could have been made against most foreign caravans. Merchants frequently did act as spies, bringing back valuable information about the political situation in distant countries, the readiness of troops, and the morale of the populace. Genghis Khan, like many leaders of the time, used merchants to spread propaganda about him—to tell tales of his invincible army. Historians, however, believe the governor acted under orders from the shah to incite the anger of Genghis Khan.

An Invitation to War

Seeking compensation for this loss of life and property, Genghis Khan sent three representatives to the shah's court. They demanded that the shah hand the governor over to the Mongols so they could punish him. But the Khwarazm Shah refused. He had one of the khan's envoys killed and burned the beards off of the other two. This was a reprehensible act, since ambassadors were supposed to be treated with the utmost respect. Genghis interpreted the behavior, correctly, as an invitation to war.

Genghis Khan was outraged when he had heard of the fate of his envoys. He climbed to the top of a hill, bared his head, and prayed to the Eternal Blue Heaven for three days. "I was not the author of this trouble," he said, "grant me the strength to exact vengeance."[26] When he came down, he was ready to begin his invasion.

4 Expanding the Empire

After the Mongols' invasion, the world seemed as tangled as the hair of an Ethiopian. Men were like wolves.

> Sa'di, Persian poet
> (1213–1291) living in the
> Khwarazm Shah's empire

Genghis Khan's expedition against the Khwarazm Shah was historically unique: For the first time, a chief of state from east Asia was personally leading an invasion of western Asia. This conflict, which would rage for five years, brought the two regions into unprecedented contact with each other.

Around 1218, as Genghis Khan began to plan his expedition against the Khwarazm Shah, the largest and most ambitious military campaign he had ever envisioned, he called a *quriltai* of his senior generals. At this *quriltai* Genghis named his successor. On the advice of one of his wives, Genghis, then about fifty-six, had agreed to choose his successor in the event of his demise during the upcoming conflict. Since the Mongols had no dynastic tradition, a cousin or brother was as likely to succeed as a son. But Genghis had created unity on the steppe to raise the position of his family, and he wanted one of his sons to succeed him. Despite his eldest son's military prowess, Genghis did not choose Jochi because he was not certain

that he was his true son, since his mother, Borte, had been captured and raped by the Merkits shortly after her marriage to Genghis. In his stead, Genghis chose his third son, Ogodei, who was known for his intelligence and inventiveness. Then Genghis made his other sons promise that they would not challenge Ogodei's right to succeed. With the question of his immediate heir resolved, Genghis concentrated on planning their campaign.

The Calm Before the Storm

A call was put out on the steppe, and thousands of herdsmen were ordered to report to Genghis's *ordus*. Between 150,000 and 200,000 men were amassed, the largest muster of Mongol power yet, but this was still less than half the size of the Khwarazm Shah's army. Genghis asked the Tangut leader for the troops he had promised to provide when the need arose, but the king told him that if he didn't have enough soldiers then he didn't deserve to be khan. This insult was later avenged.

Troops from Han China and the Uighurs added to the Mongol ranks, but since they were still outnumbered, Genghis and his advisers devised a novel strategy.

Genghis Khan (center) divides his empire among his four sons (right) in this detail from an Indian manuscript. Ogodei, Genghis's third son, was chosen as the ruling heir.

They planned to attack the shah's empire on several fronts simultaneously to confuse the enemy and make the shah believe the Mongols possessed a larger army than they did. Genghis divided his army into four corps. The first corps was led by Genghis and his senior general Subedei; the second corps was headed by his sons Ogodei and Chagadei; the third corps was led by Jebei, another senior general who, along with Subedei, had been with Genghis since the days of the tribal wars; and the fourth army was led by Genghis's oldest son, Jochi. The four corps would each be assigned a front and would play a significant role in the invasion.

When the corps went on the march, they were a formidable sight. Each *tumen* was equipped with packhorses who walked behind the ranks carrying additional equipment and weapons. In the rear of the army, behind the siege engines and reserves, was the main baggage train of camels and wagons loaded with supplies and equipment. Fully assembled tents, mobile yurts, were also carried on carts. Following the carts were the flocks of sheep and goats that provided food and milk for the armies.

Arousing Fear

Through his spies, Genghis had learned that many of the Khwarazm Shah's feudal lords had been imprisoned, deposed, or killed. He also knew that the masses had been subjected to heavy taxation and religious persecution under the shah's rule. Genghis tried to use the anger and mistrust among the nobility to his advantage, and he exploited the common people's fears in order to prevent them from resisting the Mongol attack. Genghis's operatives circulated false letters at the shah's court, stating the readiness of the shah's lords to side with the Mongols. When the Khwarazm Shah saw these letters, it reinforced his mistrust of the nobles and their military commanders. The shah became afraid to assign his armies to a single commander, for if the army were victorious, the commander might turn against him. As a result, the shah spread out his forces, and the numerically weaker Mongols, whose loyalty to Genghis was unquestionable, were able to defeat the shah's armies in the field one by one.

Vengeance upon Utrar

But Genghis was not satisfied with defeating the shah's armies. His vengeance prompted him to plunder and destroy as much as he could in an effort to topple the shah's empire. Led by Genghis's sons Chagadei and Ogodei, one corps of fifty thousand Mongol troops besieged the city of Utrar, where the merchant caravan had been executed. It took five months before the walls of the city gave way, and it was another month before the Mongols could take the citadel, where the troops and most of the citizenry had sought refuge. Through the use of mangonels (catapults), which fired hundred-pound rocks and flaming naphtha—made from a mixture of petroleum, sulfur, and potassium nitrate

sure to burn persistently—holes were eventually made in the city's defensive walls.

Utrar put up a good fight, even for the Mongols, who were adept at siege warfare. The Mongols slaughtered almost all of Utrar's inhabitants, but they were under orders from Genghis to take the governor, Inalchuq, alive. Inalchuq was held responsible for the deaths of the merchants and envoys. Knowing they were doomed, Inalchuq and his wife refused to give up, and when the citadel fell they climbed to the roof of the armory, where the governor's wife wrenched off bricks for him to hurl at their pursuers. Demolishing the building on whose roof they sat, the Mongols ultimately captured Inalchuq. The governor was executed. Utrar was utterly destroyed.

The Conquest of Bukhara

While Utrar was under attack, another corps of the Mongol army, twenty thousand horsemen under the leadership of Jebei, had moved south with orders to remove any threats from that direction and head toward Transoxiana, the central Asian region north of the Oxus River in present day Uzbekistan, Turkmenistan, and Kazakhstan. Jochi's corps were ordered to follow Jebei's corps and then branch off to attack the Khwarazm Shah's garrisons at the city of Khojend. And with the remaining corps Genghis and Subedei set their sights on Bukhara, a major economic and intellectual center of the empire.

Bukhara, whose name derives from *bukhar*, which means "center of learning," was "the cupola of Islam" or the jewel of the Persian Empire. Here doctors and philosophers, artisans and astronomers, students and teachers gathered. Situated along the Silk Road, Bukhara was a tempting prize. A successful takeover could reward Genghis's empire with knowledge and technology.

Led by Genghis and Subedei, the first corps of the army left Mongolia for Transoxiana, headed west, then disappeared. According to one source, "It was as if they had ridden off the map."[27] Actually, Genghis and Subedei were leading their army on a secret route through the Kizil Kum Desert toward the northeast border of the Khwarazm Shah's territory. The route was thought to be impassable, and the shah was not expecting an advance on this barren front. Although his spies had informed him of the other armies, the shah was completely unaware of this corps' existence. In March of 1220 Genghis's army emerged four hundred miles behind the enemy lines. Residents of Bukhara sighted the advancing columns of Mongol horsemen—"more numerous than ants or locusts"—with disbelief. Stunned, twenty thousand garrison troops stormed out of the city's gates and attempted to fight their way through the approaching Mongols. They were all killed. The plain became, in the words of one witness, "a tray filled with blood."[28] Upon the slaughter of their troops, the people of Bukhara opened the gates to their city and let the Mongols in.

Thinking that it was the sultan's palace, Genghis rode into the largest Muslim temple and ordered that it be con-

Mongol troops lay siege to Bukhara, one of the Persian Empire's most coveted cities.

The Destruction of Bukhara

In The History of the World Conqueror, *translated by J. A. Boyle, Persian historian Ata-Malik Juvaini describes the Mongol destruction of the city of Bukhara (referred to here as Bokhara), which had been a citadel of learning and culture.*

"Khans, leaders, and notables, who were the chief men of the age and the favourites of the Sultan [Islamic ruler] and who in their glory would set their feet on the head of Heaven, now became the captives of abasement and were drowned in the sea of annihilation. . . .

Of the [populace] no male was spared who stood higher than the butt of a whip and more than thirty thousand were counted amongst the slain; whilst their small children, the children of their nobles and their womenfolk, slender as the cypress, were reduced to slavery. . . . Now one man had escaped from Bokhara after its capture and had come to [the city of] Khorasan. He was questioned about the fate of that city and replied: 'They came, they sapped, they burnt, they slew, they plundered and they departed.' Men of understanding who heard this description were all agreed that in the Persian language there could be nothing more concise than this speech."

verted into a stable. Cases that held manuscripts of the Koran, the Muslim holy book, were dumped out and filled with grain, and horses ate where the religious texts had been housed. Genghis addressed the people, describing the treachery of the shah, and said, "I am the punishment of God. If you had not committed great sins, God would not have sent a punishment like me upon you."[29]

While the Mongols were plundering Bukhara, taking cartloads of goods and enslaving women and children, a fire swept through the closely packed wooden houses of the city. Soon stone structures were all that remained of the once grand city. Prisoners were taken, but many of the residents were allowed to flee into the countryside, where they could pass along the tale of the most recent Mongol conquest.

The Fall of Samarkand

The Mongols hoped that the residents of Samarkand, their next target, would hear the stories and submit without a fight. Setting out for Samarkand, the shah's capital, Genghis forced the prisoners from Bukhara to march ahead of the Mongol army. As they neared the city in modern-day Uzbekistan, their numbers made the army seem even larger, and the prisoners provided a human shield against enemy arrows. Having heard of Samarkand's

The victorious Mongol army approaches Samarkand, the cosmopolitan capital of the Khwarazm Shah. The Mongols destroyed the city and either killed or enslaved the population.

defenses, the Mongols had been prepared for a long siege, but the city fell in just five days. The invaders had never seen a city as cosmopolitan or as lavish as Samarkand, with its exotic fruits and merchandise. Everything of value was taken.

The fate of the citizens depended on their vocation: All of Samarkand's soldiers were put to death. The Mongols raped the women and then kept or sold them as slaves. Clerics and other holy men were spared. All of the artisans and craftsmen in the city were transported back to Karakorum in Mongolia, where they would serve at Genghis's court. Records indicate that after the Mongol invasion in 1220, the population of Samarkand dropped by 75 percent.

One skilled person presumed to have been taken by the Mongols after Samarkand was conquered was Ata-Malik Juvaini, a twenty-seven-year-old Persian man from the empire of the Khwarazm Shah. Juvaini was eventually brought to Karakorum, where, in the 1250s, he was encouraged to write a history of the Mongol conquests. Today Juvaini's *The History of the World Conqueror* is a valuable source of information about the Mongol Empire. Perhaps because he is in the service of the Mongols, Juvaini supports the belief that the Mongols were on a mission from heaven. Showing his familiarity with the Christian tradition, which had its representatives at the Mongol court, Juvaini suggests that the Mongols themselves are the horsemen of the apocalypse:

There has been transmitted to us a tradition of the traditions of God which says "these are my horsemen; through them I shall avenge me on those that rebelled against me," nor is there a shadow of a doubt but that these words are a reference to the horsemen of [Genghis] Khan and to his people.[30]

Like many whose countries were invaded by the Mongols, Juvaini compared the Mongols' victory to the punishment of God.

Hunting for the Shah and His Son

The Khwarazm Shah managed to flee Samarkand before the Mongols arrived, so Genghis sent Subedei and Jebei after him while he and his youngest son, Tolui, pursued the shah's son, the sultan Jalal al-Din, who had also escaped the city. For nearly a year Subedei and Jebei chased the shah from province to province, but the shah eventually died from ill health before they could capture him. This search turned into one of the largest reconnaissance missions in history when Jebei and Subedei reached the Caspian Sea. Deciding they wanted to know what lay beyond to the west, Jebei and Subedei and twenty thousand horsemen continued their journey. Living off the land and acquiring fresh horses through battle, the group beat two armies in Georgia and crossed the Caucasus Mountains in winter, defeating a band of Turkish tribes on the Russian steppe. The Russians spread an alarm throughout the principalities and managed to raise an army of eighty thousand to challenge the foreign invaders, but it was no match for the Mongols.

The Russian people knew nothing about the Mongols, including where they had come from. "Unknown tribes came," recorded a Russian monk, "none knows who they are or whence they came—nor what their language is, nor of what race they are nor what their faith is—God alone knows who they are and whence they came out."[31] When Jebei and Subedei returned to Genghis on the central Asian steppe, they had ridden eight thousand miles and accomplished what was arguably one of the greatest cavalry feats in history. Unfortunately for the Russians, they had not seen the last of the Mongols.

The Destructive Path of Pursuit

The shah's son, Jalal al-Din, continued to evade capture for years, and he made several attempts to raise armies of resisters. As the Mongols chased him through the remnants of the shah's empire, destroying cities in the process, Jalal al-Din became enshrined in Persian literature as a figure of heroic importance.

Genghis did not want to leave any cities intact to harbor his enemies, so while he and Tolui, who was known for his cruelty, pursued Jalal al-Din, they moved their army in a destructive, tornado-like path through what is now Iran, Afghanistan, and Pakistan. Persian chronicles report the destruction of cities like Merv, where Tolui had more than seven hundred thousand put to death, sparing only eighty craftsmen. According to Juvaini, however, after the carnage of Merv, the holy man 'Izz-ad-Din Nassaba and his helpers passed thirteen days and nights in counting the people slain within the town. Taking into account only those that were plain to see and leaving aside those that had been killed in holes and cavities and in the villages and deserts, they arrived at a figure of more than one million three hundred thousand.[32]

Other cities, such as Nishapur and Balkh suffered similar fates, devastations that permanently hindered their development and denied them their former glory. The city of Herat was initially spared when the Mongols first occupied it in 1221, but when the citizens later rose up against the invaders, the Mongols slaughtered the inhabitants without mercy. Though Jalal al-Din was never caught, his people paid a heavy price.

The Aftermath of War

Before returning to Mongolia, Genghis Khan arranged the administration of the conquered lands, installing governors who

Genghis Khan consults the fates in this Chinese illustration. For matters pertaining to mortality and religion, the aging khan called upon the wisdom of the Taoist sage Ch'ang-Ch'un.

would act as his personal representatives in the cities and arranging systems of taxation and tax collection. The Mongols' failure to set up an effective presence in northern China following their initial victory over the Chin had only made it easy for the enemy to recover conquered land, and the Mongols had learned from their mistakes. The garrisons left behind in the conquered territories were not large, but given the decreased populations and the fear of the Mongols in these cities, they were sufficient. Genghis also summoned the Taoist sage Ch'ang-Ch'un from China and, perhaps conscious of his impending death, consulted with him on matters of mortality and religion. Genghis had hoped in vain that Ch'ang-Ch'un, who was over seventy and renowned for his old age, might possess some secret to longevity. Genghis listened to the holy man's advice about how he ought to rule the people and allow for religious toleration, and he had Ch'ang-Ch'un's instructions written down.

In 1225, seven years after they had first set out against the Khwarazm Shah, Genghis and his men returned to Mongolia, marching the long lines of acquired slaves alongside the caravans full of other war booty—gold, jewels, silk, and coins of all kinds. Despite the enormous riches he accumulated through his many raids, Genghis frowned upon luxury and, unlike his successors, his change in circumstances did not affect his lifestyle.

Repaying Old Debts

There were important matters waiting for Genghis's attention at home. Since the general in charge of the Mongols'

provinces in China had died, the Chin had managed to regain control of the territory Genghis had wrested from them years before, so the Mongols would need to retake China. Genghis also needed to take his revenge on the Tangut king who had snubbed him by refusing to supply troops for the western Asia campaign.

In 1226 Genghis, now approximately fifty-nine, directed his attention toward the Tanguts. The Mongols devised ingenious methods to carry out their revenge. For instance, they dammed up rivers and then let them loose, flooding entire Tangut cities. The Mongols' battlefield tactics were also characterized by inventiveness. During a battle on the frozen Yangtze River, the Mongols scattered grit on their side of the ice and tied felt underneath their horses' hooves, and thus defeated the slipping, skidding Tanguts.

Early in the Tangut campaign Genghis was thrown from his horse and suffered severe internal injuries. Although his doctors advised him to stay away from the battlefield until he recovered, Genghis insisted that he would stay with his army until they were victorious over the Tanguts. While Genghis was recovering from his fall, his son Jochi died. Rumors circulated that he had secretly been poisoned. Jochi had quarreled with his father and brothers over the conduct of the war in western Asia, vehemently disagreeing with the carnage and destruction they brought on these lands. It is possible that Genghis was behind his death. Jochi was considered disloyal, and Genghis may have feared that disagreement between his sons would undermine the unity of the empire. According to one account, though, upon the news of Jochi's death, Genghis retired to his tent and grieved for three days.

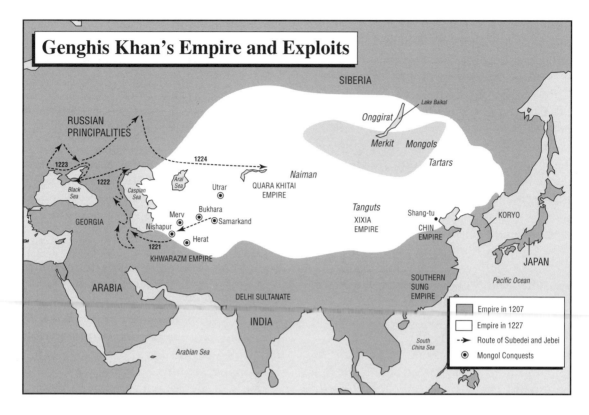

Genghis Khan's Empire and Exploits

SIBERIA

Lake Baikal

RUSSIAN PRINCIPALITIES

Onggirat

Merkit   Mongols

Tartars

1223

1224

Naiman

1222

Aral Sea

Black Sea

Caspian Sea

Utrar

QUARA KHITAI EMPIRE

GEORGIA

Merv

Bukhara

Samarkand

Nishapur

1221

Herat

KHWARAZM EMPIRE

ARABIA

DELHI SULTANATE

INDIA

Arabian Sea

Tanguts

XIXIA EMPIRE

Shang-tu

CHIN EMPIRE

SOUTHERN SUNG EMPIRE

KORYO

JAPAN

Pacific Ocean

South China Sea

Empire in 1207
Empire in 1227
Route of Subedei and Jebei
Mongol Conquests

Before the end of the Tangut campaign, Genghis, still recovering, contracted what may have been typhus or malaria. With his remaining sons, he discussed how to finish the war with the Tanguts. His sons also vowed that they would take revenge next on the Chin. When he neared death, Genghis shouted, "My descendants will wear gold, they will eat the choicest meats, they will ride the finest horses, they will hold in their arms the most beautiful women and they will forget to whom they owe it all."[33]

The Death of the World Conqueror

In August of 1227, when he was over sixty years old, Genghis Khan, the uniter of the tribes, emperor of the Mongols, died. Genghis had chosen to be buried under Mount Burkhan Kaldun, near the Onon River, where the Mongols' totemic ancestors, the blue wolf and the fallow doe, were said to have mated. Every living thing that met with his funeral train on its way to the mountain was killed, so that they might serve Genghis in the next world. At the final resting place, legend claims that forty bejeweled slave girls and forty beautiful horses were sacrificed and buried beside Genghis, then thousands of horsemen rode over the burial site to disguise it. To this day, Genghis Khan's burial site has never been found.

At the time of his death, the land that Genghis Khan had vanquished was four times the size of Alexander the Great's empire and twice the size of the Roman Empire. Yet Genghis had never been as interested in the annexation of territories as part of their conquest. The Mongols would vanquish the enemy, take all of their possessions, and depart, leaving only a few followers to collect taxes. Genghis had founded a dynasty, and he hoped that his sons and their descendants would carry it on after his death. But to do this, they would need to create an administration capable of maintaining the vast holdings of the Mongol nation. The creation of this administration would ultimately lead the Mongol nobility away from their nomadic roots toward a more sedentary imperial lifestyle.

Ogodei Becomes Khan

As Genghis had requested, his son Ogodei succeeded him as emperor in a *quriltai* held in 1229. Genghis's four heirs—Jochi (now dead but represented by his sons), Chagadei, Ogodei, and Tolui—became known as the Golden Clan, the ruling aristocracy, and only they (and their descendants) maintained the right to succeed as khan. When he selected Ogodei as ruling heir, Genghis also designated large *ulus*, tracts of territory over which to rule, to each of his sons. Each *ulu* consisted of land where nomads dwelled and included an army, animals, and a staff of artisans. The holder of the *ulu* was also entitled to a share of the entire empire's tax revenue. Genghis also designated *ulus* for his most honored commanders and supporters, though the largest *ulus* went to his sons.

Under Mongol tradition, the eldest son was given the lands farthest from home. Since Genghis's oldest son, Jochi, had already died, two of Jochi's sons, Orda and Batu, received the lands "to the west as far as the hoof of a Mongol horse had trod," and these leaders and their lineages ruling the territories near Russia became known as the White Horde and the Golden Horde, respectively. Genghis's son Chagadei received land in central Asia that had belonged to the Quara Khitai, and Ogodei was given the land northeast of Chagadei's. Tolui received the Mongol heartland, near the Onon River, the traditional inheritance of the youngest son.

The Wisdom of Yeh-lu Ch'u-ts'ai

The first action Ogodei took as emperor was to carry out his father's desire to reconquer the Chin, which he did with the help of the Sung Empire in southern China. Ogodei also began to build a more effective administration to govern Mongol lands. Ogodei acted upon the advice of the Khitan astrologer Yeh-lu Ch'u-ts'ai, whose family had worked in the Chin court.

When he was first brought to him as a prisoner, Genghis took Yeh-lu Ch'u-ts'ai into his court, enlisting him to help recruit other talented Chin and Khitan prisoners. Genghis had admired Yeh-lu Ch'u-ts'ai and consulted him on matters of importance. Upon Genghis Khan's death, Ogodei inherited the astrologer. It was Yeh-lu Ch'u-ts'ai who persuaded Ogodei not to slaughter all the Chin in northern China after the Mongol victory. Though Subedei and others wanted to clear the land of previous tenants so it could be used by Mongol herdsmen, Yeh-lu Ch'u-ts'ai argued that tax revenues and harvest contributions would benefit the empire more than pastureland.

Creating an Administration

Under Genghis, Yeh-lu Ch'u-ts'ai had developed a mobile civil service, rescuing books from wherever the Mongols traveled and saving libraries from destruction. For his useful advice on matters of taxation, he was allowed to expand the administrative capabilities of the civil service under Ogodei. To ensure that Mongol leadership in the conquered territories would be effective, a group of men called *darughachi* were selected to act as provincial military governors. The Mongols borrowed the idea of the *darughachi* from the Khitans, who had used it to organize their conquered territories. The *darughachi* were

After succeeding his father on the throne, Ogodei (center) established a permanent capital for the Mongol Empire in Karakorum.

chosen from the ranks of the *keshig*, the most trusted bodyguards of the Great Khan. They were in direct communication with the khan and could be relied on to carry out orders. The *darughachi* ensured that the subject community did not go back on its promise of submission to the Mongols, and they were also responsible for collecting and forwarding taxes from the subject population to Mongolia.

A Permanent Capital

To help expedite the delivery of tribute and streamline the budding administration, Ogodei decided to construct an official center of activity and create a permanent capital for the empire. The traditional nomad encampment of yurts and tents was insufficient to meet the demands posed by the new empire. Foreign heads of state were constantly visiting or paying tribute, and ambassadors were traveling back and forth to all reaches of the empire. Although Genghis had wanted the empire to remain based on the nomad lifestyle, Ogodei was more open to new ideas and foreign practices. He created a permanent capital at Karakorum, which was not part of the Mongols' original territory but was located approximately halfway between Ogodei's and Tolui's *ulus* in the part of Mongolia that was formerly Naiman territory. The site was a crossroads where merchants' caravans and migrating nomads had intersected for centuries, and Ogodei envisioned it as the political and commercial hub of the empire.

Karakorum was constructed as a walled city with a compound for Ogodei and his court, quarters for merchants and the court's Chinese artisans, and an area for the administration's treasury and revenue gathering service. Since the Mongols preferred to sleep outdoors, they erected their tents outdoors in a circular pattern within the palace compound. Although Ogodei continued to migrate seasonally, the city of Karakorum provided a convenient place to house the empire's administration and to hold court.

While Ogodei was working to construct a more effective administration, he continued to face problems created by the lack of organization in the territories.

Just as the Chin had managed to regain power during the Mongols' campaign in western Asia, Jalal al-Din had managed to form a powerful resistance force in the shah's old territories while the Mongols were rebattling the Chin. In 1230 Ogodei sent an army, led by the Mongol general Chormaghun, to put down the restored Khwarazm sultanate, and Jalal al-Din was once again chased out of his homeland, eluding capture but never managing to raise any supporters again. Chormaghun remained as the *darughachi*, or military governor, in these reconquered territories, and over a period of ten years he conquered many of the neighboring small states of the Caucasus, working his way to the kingdom of Georgia by 1236. Another *darughachi* was sent to help control western Asia. By strengthening their control in this region, the Mongols paved the way for further westward expansion.

The *Quriltai* of 1235

Returning from the successful invasion of the Chin in 1234, Ogodei arrived in

The Mongol Capital at Karakorum

To centralize the government and provide a place for visiting ambassadors, Ogodei decided to build a capital for the Mongol Empire in Karakorum, Mongolia, halfway between the ulus *of Chagadei and Tolui. In the thirteenth century a French missionary, Friar William of Rubruck, visited this capital (which he called Caracorum). He left a description in his manuscript "The Journey of William of Rubruck," which has been published in editor Christopher Dawson's* Mission to Asia.

"As for the city of Caracorum I can tell you that, not counting the [khan's] palace, it is not as large as the village of Saint Denis, and the monastery of Saint Denis is worth ten times more than that palace. There are two districts there: the Saracens' [Muslim] quarter where the markets are, and many merchants flock thither on account of the court which is always near it and on account of the number of envoys. The other district is that of the Cathayans [Chinese] who are all craftsmen. Apart from these districts there are the large palaces of the court scribes. There are twelve pagan temples belonging to the different nations, two mosques in which the law of Mahomet [Islam] is proclaimed, and one church for the Christians at the far end of the town. The town is surrounded by a mud wall and has four gates. At the east gate are sold millet and other grain, which is however seldom brought there; at the west sheep and goats are sold; at the south oxen and carts; at the north horses."

A large stone tortoise, a symbol of good luck, is one of the few remains of Karakorum.

The stone walls of Karakorum, site of the ancient capital of Mongolia. The creation of a capital helped transition the nomadic Mongols into a more sedentary society.

Mongolia to find the construction of Karakorum still under way. He called the Golden Clan and their advisers to a *quriltai* in 1235 so they could assess the state of the empire and make plans for the future. Yeh-lu Ch'u-ts'ai managed to convince Ogodei that "although the empire had been conquered on horseback, it would not be ruled on horseback." [34] Guided by Yeh-lu Ch'u-ts'ai, the Mongols began to make the transition from a nomadic existence to a more sedentary one. Yeh-lu Ch'u-ts'ai took advantage of the *quriltai* to push his ideas for tax reform, the running of the Mongol royal court, the establishment of libraries, and the creation of schools where Mongol children could be trained as future civil administrators. Ogodei heeded the adviser's words and implemented these novel changes.

Ogodei also improved the empire's communications network, known as the Yam, by ordering the construction of staging posts throughout the empire and between all of the *ulus*, especially between the residences of Ogodei, Chagadei, and Batu. Under this new order, wells were dug at regular intervals to supply messengers with water, and grain, horses, and food for the riders were supplied to all of the staging stations, which were located a day's riding distance apart. Official messengers

This thirteenth century Mongol passport, or paiza, *ensured messengers and diplomats safe passage through Mongol lands.*

were also given a *paiza*, a kind of identification badge that guaranteed them safe passage and assistance.

While discussing the future of the empire at the 1235 *quriltai*, the Golden Clan received reports that General Chormaghun was making progress in the conquest of the kingdom of Georgia. The success of this campaign influenced the direction in which the Golden Clan decided to expand the empire. Jochi's son Batu, who led the westernmost *ulu*, reported that there were great opportunities in western lands—including those which Subedei had traveled through during his pursuit of the Khwarazm Shah. Since the westernmost territories were also the weakest link in the Mongol chain, Subedei suggested that they send troops to bolster these areas and then begin a campaign farther west into Europe, attacking one nation at a time. The Golden Clan warmed to this idea, and Ogodei suggested that he lead the western campaign himself. But Yeh-lu Ch'u-ts'ai reminded Ogodei that times were different now than in Genghis's day. He insisted that, as khan, Ogodei's place was in Karakorum, directing the empire. Since Genghis had given Batu the westernmost lands, the Golden Clan decided that Batu should lead the expedition into Europe—a venture Subedei mistakenly believed might take as long as eighteen years to accomplish.

5 East Meets West

Before the Mongol army attacked Europe, they sent out a network of spies to gather information about the political situations in the countries they planned to invade. In contrast, the Europeans knew virtually nothing of the Mongols when they first appeared; they were termed the "unknown tribes." The steppe land east of the Ural Mountains was a great unknown to Europe. Although trade routes connected east and west, and the Crusades had introduced Christians and Muslims in the Holy Land, there was little cultural exchange going on between east Asia and Europe. As a result, one historian has compared the arrival of Mongols in Europe to an invasion by extraterrestrials.

The Mongol Invasion of Eastern Europe

The first step in the Mongol invasion of Europe was to secure all of the land leading up to the banks of the Volga River, which was then the easternmost boundary of Russia and the gateway to Europe. As the Mongols passed through the lands leading up to the Volga, they subjugated the tribes they encountered and gathered many new conscripts for their army. In ad-

dition to Mongol horsemen and subjugated tribesmen, the army for the European expedition included several corps of Chinese and Persian engineers who were needed to construct siege equipment. The army was led by Batu and among the ranks were ten princes from the Golden Clan, including Batu's brothers and the sons of Chagadei, Ogodei, and Tolui. By the winter of 1237, the army of 120,000 had cleared the eastern territories and was prepared to cross the frozen Volga into Russia.

Subedei's plan was for the Mongol army to quickly drive into Russia, dividing the dozen principalities of the region in order to reduce the chance of a united Russian opposition. Through their spies, the Mongols knew the most powerful of the Russian princes were Prince Michael of Kiev and Grand Duke Yuri of Suzdal, and their plan was to wedge the Mongol forces in between the two.

After crossing the Volga, the Mongols rode north through forested country to disguise their arrival. When they neared the province of Riazan in eastern Russia, they sent a female ambassador ahead with two escorts. The woman spoke the language of the Russian people; she told them about the Mongols and demanded that they surrender, submit to a tax, and provide reinforcements for the Mongol army. When the prince of Riazan scoffed at the strange woman's order, the Mongols began to cut down the trees near the city to construct a stockade. The prince was reluctant to send his troops into the field, so the Mongol stockade eventually encircled the city's walls.

The Mongols had become accomplished siege warriors during their long campaigns in China and Persia. They used catapults to fire rocks or burning tar at gates and walls. From the Khwarazm Shah's army they had captured lightweight catapults with a long range, and enormous crossbows, called ballistas, that could launch projectiles a great distance. During their war with the Chin, they had also encountered explosives, both rockets and grenades (clay pods packed with explosives that were thrown by catapult and by hand). The Mongols always incorporated new inventions into their army, and they used the combination of catapulted rocks, burning tar, flaming naphtha, grenades, and firebombs to destroy enemy fortifications.

Safe behind their stockade, the Mongols fired artillery at Riazan for five days until the defenses were breached. The city was then taken and most of the inhabitants

As the Mongols conquered new lands, they incorporated subjugated people into their army, as this Japanese scroll painting from 1283 illustrates.

murdered, including the entire royal family. The Riazan massacre was meant to be an example for the other principalities. As was the Mongol custom, a few survivors were allowed to flee so that the news of the disaster would spread.

Other Russian principalities were similarly devastated. Even Kiev and Suzdal fell to Mongol might, and news of the terror spread to the coast of northern Europe. According to a Russian account of the attack on Kiev, the Mongols were merciless.

> The inhabitants were, without regard to age or sex, slaughtered with the savage cruelty of the Mongol revenge; some were impaled, some shot at with arrows for sport, others were flayed or had nails or splinters driven under their nails. Priests were roasted alive, and nuns and maidens were ravished in the churches before their relatives. No eye remained open to weep for the dead.[35]

Although the Mongols seemed invincible to outsiders, they were in fact experiencing some internal rivalries. As more and more western territory was added to the empire, a rift began to grow between Batu and the rest of the Golden Clan. Genghis Khan had bequeathed Batu all of the westernmost lands, and now his personal realm was rapidly expanding, increasing his wealth and status, while the other clan territories remained the same. The other minor khans grew jealous of Batu and his horde, which was expanding with the resources and manpower of the entire Mongol army.

After leaving 30,000 troops behind to maintain control in Russia, the Mongols, with a remaining force of 130,000, prepared to push into Hungary, which Subedei had determined was the strongest realm and thus a main objective in the campaign to conquer eastern Europe. Before attacking Hungary, the Mongols divided their army into smaller units so that some troops might attack at many points along a six-hundred-mile front, while others could be used to obliterate any potential threats from Hungary's neighbors. Twenty thousand Mongol horsemen, for example, were sent to Poland with instructions to defeat any threat from that nation or from Lithuania to the north. Subedei did not want Polish or Lithuanian forces to interfere in his Hungarian campaign. Meanwhile, the majority of the army would cross the Carpathian mountain range into Hungary and engage the Hungarian king's army. Once the Mongol contingents in Poland and Lithuania had removed all threats, they were to converge in Hungary and assist with its defeat.

Comparing the Armies

The Mongol army was the most superior fighting force in the world. More advanced than any army of the time, the Mongols were a formidable enemy for the armies of Europe.

The key to the Mongol horseman's success was his mobility—his lightweight armor allowed his mount to run quickly and allowed him to shift and pivot in the saddle, shooting arrows from in front or from behind. In contrast, the western and eastern European knight in the first half of the thirteenth century wore heavy steel mail armor over most of his body and a bucket-shaped helmet. The knight placed his own weight, plus over one hundred

European knights charge into battle during the Crusades. These heavily armored soldiers were no match for the extremely mobile Mongols.

pounds in armor and gear, onto his horse's back; as a result, the knight's mobility was restricted. European combat tended to be face-to-face, ending with an on-the-ground duel once both combatants were knocked off of their horses. The Mongols, on the other hand, preferred to remain mounted, using the agility of their horses to gain the advantage over their slower opponents.

European armies relied heavily on foot soldiers, but these were often poorly trained peasants who had been pressed into service. The chain of command was not clear, and channels of communication were poor. This was in sharp contrast to the Mongol war machine, in which each soldier acted as part of a formation that performed practiced maneuvers. The Mongols used intelligence to uncover enemy plans and positions, and they employed a system of flags and messengers to

convey information from a distance to commanders in the field.

Against the armies of Europe, the Mongols executed their traditional strategies. Mongol light cavalry would typically disrupt enemy infantry with arrows until the heavy cavalry could be brought to bear. The heavy cavalry would be summoned by the *naqara*, a huge drum carried into battle on a two-humped camel. The heavy brigade began at a walk, but at the commander's sign, the drumbeat quickened and the men broke into a trot. Then, at just the right moment, the commander would signal the drummer, who would beat a furious roll, causing the soldiers to shriek, and with lances lowered, gallop toward the enemy.

The resourceful nomads, however, also resorted to smoke screens and other unusual tactics to confuse the enemy and ensure Mongol victory. During the Battle of Dobropole in Poland, for example, a Mongol soldier caused widespread confusion and panic among the Poles by charging their front line and screaming "Run!" in Polish to the enemy soldiers. This bizarre behavior caused some in the Polish army to panic and flee, and the confusion was the turning point that resulted in a Mongol victory. Reveling in the success of the tactic, the Mongols took an ear from each of their victims. As many as nine sacks of ears were sent to Batu by his officers.

But Mongol victories were not always achieved so easily. The Hungarian army was the strongest foe the Mongols had yet faced. While the common soldier was no serious threat to the Mongols, the Hungarians had enlisted the aid of some of the best-trained foreign knights in all of Europe. During hand-to-hand combat with cavalry units composed of these knights, the Mongols took severe losses.

Battle of the River Sajo

The most decisive battle for Hungary took place near the River Sajo on April 10, 1241. Batu's army was waiting on the banks of the river for news of a final battle raging in Poland. When the word came that the Polish army was no longer a threat, Batu

This European illustration portrays the Mongol invasion of 1241. During the Mongols' foray into Europe, they encountered the formidable Hungarian army, whose skill and strength rivaled that of the invaders.

prepared to cross the river with his army and attack Hungary's King Bela from head on, while Subedei took his division north in search of another crossing point so his men could circle around and attack the Hungarians from behind.

Batu's men crossed the Sajo on a narrow stone bridge, while King Bela's forces waited on the opposite side. Since the bridge would only allow several men across at a time, the Hungarians were easily able to kill the advancing Mongols. Quickly, Batu ordered the catapults brought out and a volley of explosives were fired across at the Hungarians, who retreated far enough to allow the Mongols safe passage.

The Army That Astonished Europe

Europeans thought of the Mongols as barbarians who overran everything in their path by virtue of their sheer number. But H. G. Wells, in Volume 2 of his Outline of World History, *points out that the brilliance of the Mongol army was not fully understood in the West until the modern era.*

"It is only recently that European history has begun to understand that the successes of the Mongol army, which overran Poland and occupied Hungary in the spring of A.D. 1241, were won by consummate strategy and were not due to a mere overwhelming superiority of numbers. But this fact has not become a matter of common knowledge; the vulgar opinion which represents the Tartars [Mongols] as a wild horde carrying all before them solely by their multitude, and galloping through Eastern Europe without a strategic plan, rushing at all obstacles and overcoming them by mere weight, still prevails.

It was wonderful how punctually and effectually the arrangements of the [Mongol] commanders were carried out in operations extending from the Lower Vistula to Transylvania. Such a campaign was quite beyond the power of any European army of the time, and it was beyond the vision of any European commander. There was no general in Europe, from Frederick II downward, who was not an amateur in strategy compared to Ogodei. It should also be noticed that the Mongols embarked upon the enterprise with full knowledge of the political situation of Hungary and the condition of Poland—they had taken care to inform themselves by a well-organized system of spies; on the other hand, the Hungarians and Christian powers, like childish barbarians, knew hardly anything about their enemies."

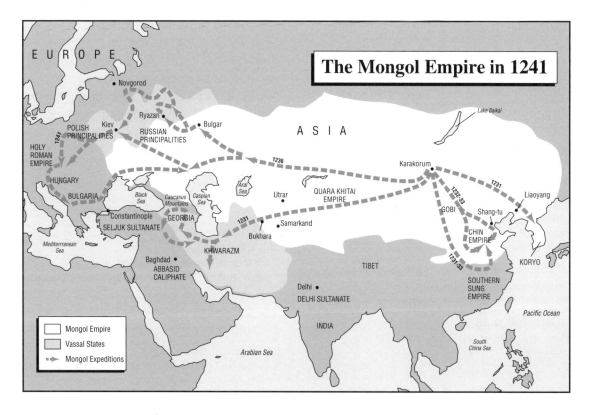

The Mongol Empire in 1241

Batu's force of forty thousand finally crossed the bridge, but they were seriously outnumbered by King Bela's army of one hundred thousand. Unfortunately for Batu, Subedei's force had been delayed when, unable to find a northern river crossing, their engineers were forced to build a makeshift bridge. Batu's force barely held their own against the Hungarians, as they tried to deflect the constant volley of head-on charges with arrows and firebombs. Batu grew desperate waiting for Subedei's army. He slowly turned his own men so that when the Hungarians pressed their attack they would keep their backs to the place at which Subedei was expected to arrive.

Just when it looked as if Subedei were never going to appear and the Hungarians would be victorious, Batu got the signal that help was near. Immediately, he ordered that his men cast out in a single line, forming a long semicircle. Although initially confused, the Hungarians quickly realized they were surrounded. Subedei's army had come in behind them, and the Mongols were closing in on them in a giant circle, like the conclusion of a hunt. Panicking, the Hungarians charged and managed to break through the circle, but Subedei's men followed them back to their fortified camp and laid siege with artillery. The encampment was devastated. Those who did manage to escape were chased down by Mongol archers, and by the end of the day sixty thousand Hungarians had been killed.

After ravaging Hungary, Batu dispatched a *tumen* into Austria, and Mongol scouts were sighted outside Vienna in 1242.

Other Mongol scouting units went to Croatia and Dalmatia; Mongol spies were also spotted within sixty miles of Venice. The Mongols were preparing to take more European territory, but before their attack they wanted to gather information and rest for a few months, allowing the herds they had brought along to graze and fatten.

Europe Braces for Another Attack

The destruction of the Christian kingdoms of Poland and Hungary was more terrifying to western Europe than the disasters that befell the eastern Orthodox Russians. Up until the attacks on Hungary and Poland, Europeans, whose knowledge of Asia was encumbered with myth and legend, had hoped there might be some chance that the Mongols were Christians. Rumors of a Christian king named Prester John, who maintained a Christian army in Asia, had long circulated in Europe. This was because, following the fall of the eastern half of the Roman Empire, the eastern Christians, or Nestorians, had been cut off from western Christianity, although their religion continued to develop. Merchants and other travelers who encountered Nestorian Christians abroad helped perpetuate the rumor of eastern Christians and of Prester John's kingdom.

But when western Europeans knew the Mongols were not a Christian army, they feared the worst: an apocalypse. Many believed the world was coming to an end. Monsters had always been rumored to live in the east, since the legend of Alexander the Great, who was supposed to have imprisoned the terrible giants, Gog and Ma-

gog, beyond the Derbent Pass in the Caucasus Mountains. In the book of Revelation, it was said that Gog and Magog would one day be released by Satan to overrun the world. Many thirteenth-century Europeans believed that day had come when they heard reports of the Mongol invasion. Fear was rampant. An excerpt from a letter sent by Count Henry of Lorraine, France, to his father in 1241 reveals the atmosphere of fear and the belief that the Mongols were the punishment of God:

> The dangers foretold long ago in Holy Scripture are now, owing to our sins, springing up and erupting. A cruel tribe of people beyond number, lawless and savage, is now invading and occupying our borders, and has now reached the land of the Poles, after roaming through many other lands and exterminating the people.[36]

Pope Gregory declared a crusade against the Mongols. Letters asking for help were sent to all the courts of Europe. The kingdoms responded not by lending troops but by stockpiling arms in castles, digging trenches, and otherwise preparing to fend off an attack.

A kind of hysteria spread, fanned by accounts of Mongol cruelty. The English chronicler Matthew Paris, who had never met a Mongol, gave this account of the coming horde:

> For touching upon the cruelty and cunning of these people, there can be no infamy [great enough]; and, in briefly informing you of their wicked habits, I will recount nothing of which I had either a doubt or mere opinion, but what I have with certainty proved and what I know. . . . The [Mongol]

chief, with his dinner guests and other [cannibals], fed upon the carcasses as if they were bread and left nothing but the bones for the vultures . . . the old and ugly women were given to the cannibals . . . as their daily allowance of food; those who were beautiful were not eaten but were suffocated by mobs of ravishers in spite of all their cries and lamentations. Virgins were raped until they died of exhaustion; then their breasts were cut off to be kept as dainties for their chiefs, and their bodies furnished an entertaining banquet for the savages.[37]

Fortunately for Europe, the Mongols soon became distracted from their mission of conquest by the struggle to determine who would succeed as the next Great Khan.

A Dynastic Struggle

As Europe was preparing for the worst in May of 1241, the Mongols received the news that Ogodei Khan had died. As suddenly as they had arrived, they packed up and returned to their homeland, withdrawing

The Mongols advance on Europe in this sixteenth-century illustration. Many Europeans believed the Mongols were savage, lawless, and the scourge of God.

completely from Europe and leaving Europeans to wonder what could have prompted such a rapid departure. Some considered it a miracle from God, while others believed the Mongols would be back. However, Ogodei's death saved much of Europe from a Mongol invasion. It also brought the Mongol dynastic struggle to a head.

When the Mongol *tumens* returned to Karakorum, they found the capital unstable. Two factions were fighting over who would succeed Ogodei as khan. Ogodei's wife, Toregene, had been ruling temporarily, since the death of her husband, and she was determined to install her own son, Guyuk, to the throne. It was even rumored that Toregene had had Ogodei poisoned. Another group, however, was anxious to place Mongke, the son of Tolui, at the head of the empire. Batu, the leader of the largest *ulu*, supported Mongke. By the time Batu and his army returned, however, Toregene had dismissed all of Ogodei's previous advisers and installed her own followers in the administration. Because Batu had not arrived earlier, Toregene had the upper hand and Guyuk was the next to rule.

Missionaries to the Mongols

While the Mongol leadership changed hands, a new pope, Innocent IV, prepared for the possibility of a Mongol return to Europe by calling a council in Lyons in 1245. Innocent invited all those from Hungary, Russia, and Poland who were informed about Mongol military practices, customs, and religions to participate in the council. Muslims in Persia, whose homeland had been ravaged by the Mongols,

also sent envoys to the pope's council at Lyons, urging European leaders to join them in a fight against the Mongols. But European leaders were more interested in allying with the Mongols against the Muslims. Pope Innocent decided to send missionaries to Mongolia in the hope of converting the Mongols to Christianity. If the Mongols could become Christian allies, they would be a powerful force against the Muslims in the Holy Land, where Christians had battled Muslims for centuries in the Crusades.

In 1245 a small company including Giovanni of Plano Carpini, a sixty-five-year-old Franciscan friar, set out with letters from Pope Innocent IV and instructions to personally deliver them to the leader of the Mongols. Carpini was a disciple of St. Francis, and he and his aides had little more than their faith to help them in this mission. Carpini knew nothing of the languages or of the geography of the regions through which he was traveling. And what he had heard of the Mongols was frightful. Once on the steppe, Carpini and his companions encountered Mongols who took them to Batu Khan's western *ulu*.

Batu decided the friar should go to Karakorum to meet Guyuk Khan in time for his inauguration. So the aged Carpini was made to ride at top speed, forced to keep up with his escorts, changing horses six times a day, in order to make it to Karakorum in time. Carpini was physically exhausted when he arrived several months later for Guyuk's coronation. Guyuk was given a translation of Carpini's letters, which contained the pope's advice that he convert to Christianity. Then Guyuk's own response for the pope was recorded in the Persian language. According to the surviving translation, Guyuk Khan said:

Guyuk Khan's Letter to Pope Innocent IV (1246)

Guyuk Khan sent Friar Giovanni of Plano Carpini back to Europe with his letter to the pope, recorded in Mission to Asia, *an anthology of missionaries' travel narratives edited by Christopher Dawson. Guyuk Khan wrote:*

"We, by the power of the eternal heaven,
Khan of the great Ulus
Our command:
This is a version sent to the great Pope, that he may know and understand in the [Muslim] tongue, what has been written. The petition of the assembly held in the lands of the Emperor [for our support], has been heard from your emissaries.

If he reaches [you] with his own report, Thous, who art the great Pope, together with all the Princes, come in person to serve us. At that time I shall make known all the commands of the Yasa. You have also said that supplication and prayer have been offered by you, that I might find a good entry into baptism. This prayer of thine I have not understood. . . . The eternal God has slain and annihilated these lands and peoples, because they have neither adhered to [Genghis Khan], nor to the Khagan, both of whom have been sent to make known God's command. . . . How could anybody seize or kill by his own power contrary to the command of God?

Though thou likewise sayest that I should become a trembling Nestorian Christian, worship God and be an ascetic, how knowest thou whom God absolves, in truth to whom He shows mercy?

Now you should say with a sincere heart: 'I will submit and serve you.' Thou thyself, at the head of all the Princes, come at once to serve and wait upon us! At that time I shall recognize your submission.

If you do not observe God's command, and if you ignore my command, I shall know you as my enemy. Likewise I shall make you understand. If you do otherwise, God knows what I know.

At the end of Jumada the second in the year 644.
The Seal"

The Journey of William of Rubruck

During his travels among the Mongols from 1253 through 1255, Friar William of Rubruck preached the Christian religion to those he met, including Mongke Khan. Friar Rubruck kept a detailed account of his journey, reprinted in Christopher Dawson's Mission to Asia.

"When we arrived among those barbarians, it seemed to me, as I have already said, as if I were stepping into another world. For after they had made us wait for a long time sitting in the shade of our carts, they surrounded us on horseback. Their first question was whether we had ever before been among them. On being told no, they began impudently to ask for some of our provisions. We gave them some of the biscuit and wine we had brought with us from the town; and when they had drunk one flagon of wine they asked for another, saying a man does not enter a house on one foot. We gave it to them, apologizing that we had but little. Then they enquired where we had come from and where we wanted to go. I spoke to them in the words I have already given, saying that we had heard of Sartach [a leader] that he was a Christian and that I wished to go to him as I had your letter to deliver to him.

Then they diligently enquired whether I was going of my own free will or whether I was being sent. I replied that nobody forced me to go, nor would I have gone if I did not wish to, therefore I was going of my own free will and also by the will of my superior. I took great care never to say that I was [Louis IX's] ambassador. Then they asked what was in the carts, whether it was gold or silver or precious garments that I was taking to Sartach. . . .

It is true that they take nothing away by force but they ask in a most ill-mannered and impudent fashion for whatever they see, and if a man gives to them, then he is the loser for they are ungrateful. In their own eyes they are the lords of the world and consider that nobody ought to refuse them anything; if he does not give and then afterwards stands in need of their aid, they serve him badly. They gave us some of their cows' milk to drink; the butter had been extracted from it and it was very sour, and is what they call *airan*. And so we left them and it seemed to me indeed as if I had escaped from the hands of devils."

How dost thou know that such words as thou speakest are with God's sanction [approval]? From the rising of the sun to its setting, all the lands have been made subject to me. Who could do this contrary to the command of God?

Noting that God's blessing was upon the Mongols, Guyuk went on to ask for the pope's submission, warning,

If you do not observe God's command, and if you ignore my command, I shall know you as my enemy. . . . If you should not believe our letters and the command of God nor hearken to our counsel then we shall know for certain that you wish to have war. After that we do not know what will happen, God alone knows.[38]

Carpini, fearful that Guyuk already had another invasion of Europe planned, refused the khan's offer to send Mongol envoys back to Europe with him. When the friar finally returned to Europe by way of Kiev, in 1247, he was greeted as if he had come back from the dead. Upon his return he met with Pope Innocent IV in Lyons to inform him of his mission.

A Second Attempt at Conversion

With no sign of a subsequent Mongol invasion, in 1253 another Franciscan friar, William of Rubruck, was dispatched by Louis IX of France on a religious mission to convert the stubborn Mongols. Rubruck

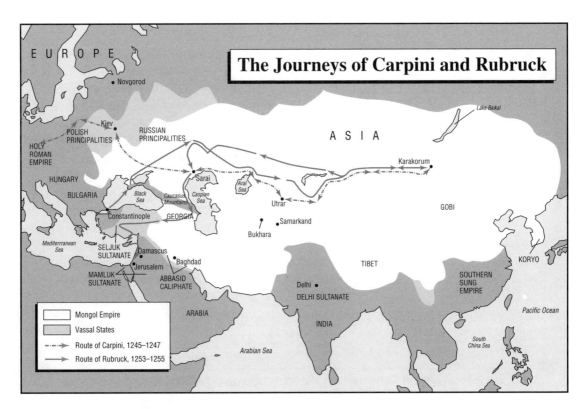

The Journeys of Carpini and Rubruck

departed from the royal court in Acre, Palestine, along with another friar, a clerk, and a translator. When he reached the first Mongol outpost and observed the customs and life of the Mongols for the first time, he wrote, "When I came among them it seemed indeed to me as if I were stepping into some other world."[39]

A Visit with Mongke

By the time William of Rubruck arrived in Karakorum, Guyuk Khan, who ruled for only two years, had already died. Following the customary regency of Guyuk's widow, Oghul-Ghaimish, Mongke had been de-

Oracle Bone Divination

William of Rubruck's travel account, published in editor Christopher Dawson's Mission to Asia, *describes the Mongol practice of oracle bone divination—a method by which they determined which course of action to take. The burning of animal scapulae and tortoise shells to divine the future was also common in ancient China. Rubruck observed oracle bone divination at Mongke Khan's residence.*

"As we were entering [Mongke's dwelling] a slave was going out, carrying away sheep's shoulder-blades which had been charred until they were as black as coal. I was greatly puzzled as to the purpose of this and when I enquired about it later I learned that the [khan] does nothing in the world without first consulting these bones; consequently he does not allow anyone to enter his dwelling until he has consulted them.

This type of divination is carried out in the following manner: when the [khan] wishes to do anything he has three of these bones brought to him before they have been burned, and holding them he thinks of that matter about which he wishes to find out whether he is to do it or not; then he hands the bones to a slave to be burned. Near the dwelling in which he is staying there are always two little buildings in which the bones are burned and every day these bones are diligently sought for throughout the encampment. When the bones, therefore, have been burned until they are black they are brought back to the [khan] and he thereupon examines them to see if with the heat of the fire they have split lengthwise in a straight line. If they have, the way is clear for him to act; if, however, the bones have cracked horizontally or round bits have shot out, then he does not do it. The bone itself or the membrane stretched over it always cracks in the fire. If, out of three, one is split in a straight line, then he acts."

clared khan. It was from Mongke Khan (referred to by Rubruck as Mangu Chan) that Rubruck learned of the Mongols' shamanistic beliefs.

On the day of Pentecost, Mangu Chan summoned me. . . . He then began to make a profession of his faith to me. "We Mongols," said he, "believe that there is but one God [Tengri, the Eternal Blue Heaven], by whom we live and by whom we die and towards Him we have an upright heart." I said, "God himself will grant this for it cannot come about but by His gift." He asked what I had said and the interpreter told him. Afterwards the Chan continued: "But just as God gave different fingers to the hand so has He given different ways to men. To you God has given the Scriptures and you Christians do not observe them. You do not find in the Scriptures that a man ought to disparage another, now do you?. . . God has given you the Scriptures and you do not keep them; to us, on the other hand, He has given soothsayers, and we do what they tell us, and live in peace."[40]

Like Carpini before him, Rubruck's attempt at converting the Mongols did not meet with much success, but he did publish an account of his travels among the Mongols, which remains one of the best sources of information on medieval Mongolia. Rubruck described Karakorum as a cosmopolitan city divided into sections for merchants, scribes, artists, scientists, and builders. He encountered merchants and craftsmen from Germany, Poland, France, Hungary, Russia, and England, all employed at the Mongol court.

Rubruck was privileged to be at the Mongol capital during a crucial time. Under Mongke's reign, the empire would expand once more, precipitating its collapse.

6 The Fracturing of Empire

Mongke Khan, grandson of Genghis, wanted to renew his grandfather's mandate of world conquest. He launched his reign with plans for two major campaigns: one against the Sung dynasty in southern China and another through Persia and into Syria, Mesopotamia, and Egypt. Mongke and his brother Kubilai planned to lead the campaign against the Sung themselves, while Mongke's brother Hulagu was put in charge of the Middle Eastern attack.

For reasons not entirely known, the Mongols lost interest in Europe, after their withdrawal in 1242, and they never again seriously considered it worthy of taking. They looked upon Persia, however, as a gold mine of learning, culture, art, science, and beauty. Baghdad was an oasis of civilization, filled with libraries of Persian and Arabian literature, a great university, and the caliph's personal treasure was one of the largest in the world. The Mongols simply could not let such a flourishing civilization exist in proximity to them without seeking its submission.

In 1255 Hulagu's army crossed the Oxus River in Central Asia. Mongol officials had been sent out months in advance to appropriate all of the pastureland in areas through which Hulagu was likely to pass. All were prohibited from grazing their cattle in these areas so the army would have grass for their horses, pack animals, and herds.

Hulagu's Army

The army was supplied with Chinese gunpowder and the latest in siege engineering equipment. Hulagu's mounted archers were led by generals who had campaigned with Subedei and Genghis Khan. His army was supplemented by a contingent of Christians from Georgia, who relished the opportunity to smite the Muslims. News of the coming of Hulagu's army prompted surrenders from the sultans, emirs, and rulers of the lands that were once the Khwarazm Shah's empire. They declared that they would offer no resistance to the traveling horde.

It was in Persia that the Mongols encountered their first obstacle: the Muslim sect known as the Assassins. The Assassins, from whom the term *assassination* derives, lived in the Elburz Mountains enclaves, and the Mongol generals and Chinese engineers had to use tremendous ingenuity to haul their artillery up the steep slopes. They were able to destroy the fortress of the Assassins' leader, Rukn ad-Din, and take him

Sorghaghtani's Influence

"At the death of each khan it was Mongol custom for the widow to rule as regent until the question of his succession had been settled; this policy provided women with a brief opportunity to exercise some influence over the direction of the empire. . . . However, by far the most influential woman at the Mongol court never actually reigned as regent.

Sorghaghtani Beki, Tolui's widow, bore him four sons before he died. . . . As time passed, it became obvious that the qualities that distinguished the sons of Tolui were entirely the result of Sorghaghtani's influence. Throughout the reigns of Ogodei and Guyuk she emerged as easily the most accomplished, learned, and certainly the wisest woman in the Mongol court, and as she aged so her importance grew. Rashid al-din, the Persian historian, described her as 'extremely intelligent and able and towered above all the women in the world.' A poet of the age waxed even more lyrically: 'If I were to see among the race of women another woman like this, I should say that the race of women was far superior to that of men!' One can only speculate how she might have directed the course of the empire had she, a lifelong Christian, managed to rule as regent. How differently might she have received the various papal envoys. But it was not to be.

Instead, Sorghaghtani devoted herself to the education and development of her four sons: Mongke, Kubilai, Hulagu, and Ariq Boke. It was her shrewd and careful maneuvering that forged an alliance with Batu Khan after Guyuk's death and ensured the election of her eldest son, Mongke, as Khan in 1251. Unfortunately, the great woman died a year later, surviving only just long enough to share in her son's triumph and to see the empire once again striving to expand. Nevertheless, her influence was felt long afterwards through the actions of her children."

prisoner. The Mongols then took Rukn ad-Din from fortress to fortress, demanding that the Assassins surrender. Whether they chose to give up without a fight or not, all of the Assassins were ultimately killed. It took the Mongols nearly two years to expunge the Assassins from their mountain enclaves, but they were victorious. In 1258 Hulagu began the march to Baghdad, the capital of the Islamic world.

The Fall of Baghdad

Hulagu sent messengers to the caliph of Baghdad to demand his surrender, but these warnings were ignored. The caliph's chief adviser, Ibn al-Alkami, a Shia Muslim, convinced the caliph that there was nothing to fear; meanwhile, motivated by the caliph's persecution of Shia Muslims, Ibn

Mongke Khan holds a feast at Karakorum in honor of his brother Hulagu's impending campaign against the Middle East.

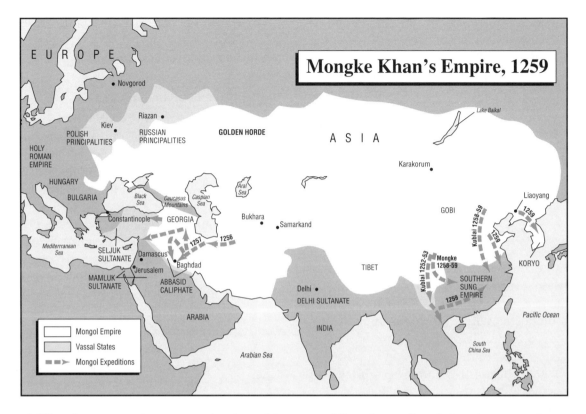

Mongke Khan's Empire, 1259

EUROPE
- Novgorod
- Riazan
- Kiev
POLISH PRINCIPALITIES
RUSSIAN PRINCIPALITIES
GOLDEN HORDE
ASIA
Lake Baikal
HOLY ROMAN EMPIRE
HUNGARY
BULGARIA
Black Sea
Caucasus Mountains
Caspian Sea
Aral Sea
Karakorum
Constantinople
GEORGIA
Bukhara
Samarkand
GOBI
Liaoyang
1259
Mediterranean Sea
SELJUK SULTANATE
Damascus
Jerusalem
Baghdad
1257 1256
MAMLUK SULTANATE
ABBASID CALIPHATE
ARABIA
TIBET
Delhi
DELHI SULTANATE
INDIA
Kublai 1258-59
Mongke 1258-59
Kublai 1252-53
1259
SOUTHERN SUNG EMPIRE
KORYO
Pacific Ocean
South China Sea
Arabian Sea

Legend:
- Mongol Empire
- Vassal States
- Mongol Expeditions

al-Alkami was secretly communicating with the Mongol army, apprising them of the pathetic state of Baghdad's defenses.

Twenty thousand troops from Baghdad's garrison had ridden out from the city to confront the enemy, but while they camped that night outside the city walls, the Mongols approached. They broke the nearby dams and dykes, flooding the encampment of Baghdad's troops. Many drowned and others, caught off guard, were killed by Mongol heavy cavalry. In the meantime, other Mongol *tumens* had been constructing a ditch and a stockade around the city, and on January 30, the bombardment began. Since the Mongol artillery supplies were three days behind schedule, the soldiers had to improvise, and they hewed rocks from nearby foundations to catapult at the city walls.

After the walls of the city came down one by one, Baghdad surrendered. On February 13, the remaining soldiers inside the city filed out, laid down their weapons, and were killed, one at a time. The caliph and his family were spared this fate. Instead, Hulagu treated the royals to a banquet and then had them sewn into Mongol carpets and trampled to death by horses. This ended the dynasty of the Abbasid caliphs, whose family had ruled from Baghdad for five hundred years. The city was pillaged. Hulagu built a treasure-house on an island in Lake Urmia to store his portion of Baghdad's spoils, which would have been cumbersome to transport on the war path.

The Mongols allowed Ibn al-Alkami to keep his position as chief minister of the city, though little remained to rule. The mosques and palaces of the city were burned, and most of the Muslim population was killed. Women and children were taken back to Karakorum, as were the contents of the caliph's treasury. According to Persian accounts, which may be slightly exaggerated, between eight hundred thousand and two million people were killed within Baghdad's walls. The Mongols were forced to leave their campsites because the smell of rotting corpses became overpowering.

Christians in the Middle East, who had lived under Muslim domination for five hundred years, heralded the Mongols as their saviors. The fall of Baghdad was regarded as a triumph by Christians. When Hulagu marched into Syria, many Christians offered allegiance and presented him with gifts. One Armenian chronicler wrote, "During the time of Baghdad's supremacy, like an insatiable bloodsucker, she had swallowed up the whole world. Now she has been punished for all the blood she has spilled and the evil she has wrought, the measure of her iniquity being filled."[41] Christians would no longer be persecuted by the powerful house of the Abbasid caliphs.

Now the only remaining sizable Islamic force that the Mongols concerned themselves with was Mamluk Egypt. Hulagu sent them the following note:

> You have heard how we have conquered a vast empire and have purified the earth of disorders which tainted it. It is for you to fly and for us to pursue, and wither will you fly, and by what road will you escape us? Our horses are swift, our arrows sharp, our swords like thunderbolts, our hearts as hard as the mountains, our soldiers as numerous

as the sand. Fortresses will not detain us, nor arms stop us; your prayers to heaven will not avail against us.[42]

Yet the Mongols never made good on this threat. In 1260 Hulagu's forces received news from riders who had been traveling on the Mongol Yam since the autumn of the previous year. They were riding to inform Hulagu that Mongke Khan was dead. While campaigning with Kubilai against the Sung in China, he had contracted dysentery and died. Immediately, Hulagu withdrew his forces and waited nearby, pondering what move to make next. Another struggle for succession was already being waged, and until a new khan was elected, the machinery of the empire would grind to a halt.

The Struggle for Succession

Mongke's brothers, Hulagu, Kubilai, and Ariq Boke, rivaled one another for the position of Great Khan. Hulagu was a great commander and had conquered Persia, and Kubilai had campaigned successfully against China and created a summer capital for the empire there. Ariq Boke had remained in the Mongol heartland, winning supporters by championing traditional Mongol values and lifestyle. In contrast, Hulagu was thought by some to have taken to the "soft" life of cities, and Kubilai was believed to have spent so much time in China that he was accused of identifying more with the Chinese than with the Mongols.

While Hulagu was just receiving word of Mongke's death and Kubilai was still fighting the Sung in China, Ariq Boke and his followers raised an army to defend his claim to succeed as khan. When the news of Mongke's death reached China, however, Kubilai, anticipating Ariq Boke's plans, called a *quriltai* of his supporters and had already declared himself khan on May 5, 1260. A civil war developed between the two factions; Hulagu, still in the Middle East, sided with Kubilai. Though he had ambitions to become Great Khan himself, Hulagu feared that if Ariq Boke succeeded he would lose the power he already had.

The Destruction of Unity

Ariq Boke turned out to be no match for Kubilai, who managed to hold on to the title. By 1264 Kubilai had defeated Ariq Boke. Although Kubilai had successfully made himself Great Khan, his position was not like that of Genghis or Ogodei or Mongke. The chain of empire was broken.

Not only was the royal lineage upset, but the empire itself was splitting into irreconcilable factions. Angered by the Mongol destruction of Islam, Berke Khan of the Golden Horde, who was a Muslim, sided with the Mamluks of Egypt and declared war on Hulagu. Hulagu was distracted from his desire to be khan and focused on fending off Berke's forces. Kubilai, the new khan, made no move to assist Hulagu but let him handle his own affairs. The *ulus* had become relatively autonomous and the empire was no longer united behind the policies of one ruler. Hulagu's Persian Ilkhanate, Ariq Boke's Chagadei khanate, and Berke's Golden Horde were beyond Kubilai's control. Instead of forcing a union, Kubilai immersed himself in the business of ruling China.

The collapse of unity within the Mongol Empire did not lead to an immediate decline. Instead, each of the *ulus* continued to exist independently. The leaders of the *ulus* had long since begun to adapt local religions, and gradually the *ulus* began to hold less and less in common. While Kubilai closely associated himself with the Buddhist church, the leaders of the western *ulus* embraced Islam. Hulagu's wife was a Christian. Through religion, marriage, and the creation of laws customized to each region, the different khanates gradually adapted themselves to the populations over which they ruled.

Throughout his life Kubilai was accused of breaking with Mongol tradition and adopting the sedentary lifestyle of the Chinese, because he surrounded himself with Chinese luxury. But Kubilai had been raised in both the Mongol and Chinese traditions; as a child many of his tutors were Chinese. Kubilai's senior wife, Chabi,

Kubilai Khan, grandson of the great Genghis Khan. During Kubilai's reign the Mongol Empire fractured into culturally different ulus.

considered many of the Mongols' policies extremely unpractical, and it was she who encouraged him to create a Mongol dynasty fashioned after the eras of the great Chinese emperors. As a result, throughout his life Kubilai's rule bridged nomadic and sedentary civilizations.

The Yuan Dynasty

In 1260 Kubilai Khan announced a new era in Asian history by declaring the Ta Yuan, or "Great Origin," dynasty of Mongol rule in China. Kubilai's Yuan dynasty would prove to be one of the most open periods in Chinese history. With Kubilai's encouragement, merchants and diplomats traveled freely between China and foreign lands. The Yuan dynasty also united China politically, bringing the southern and northern provinces of the country together.

The Mongol population in China was only a few hundred thousand, compared to the millions of Chinese. While Kubilai had Chinese advisers, he made sure that the key positions in government were all filled by Mongols, thus ensuring that Mongol interests would be protected. Kubilai invoked a strict system of racial classification when choosing government officials. Those of Mongol background were ranked highest and were most likely to hold office. Next came people of central Asian background who worked for the Mongols, and last of all were the northern and then southern Chinese, whom Kubilai did not trust.

To establish legitimacy for the dynasty Kubilai devoted time and money to creating all the trappings of an official administration. To maintain order, Kubilai created a centralized government composed of three departments: the Secretariat, which was responsible for all civil matters; the Privy Council, which handled military affairs; and the Censorate, which supervised all the government officials in the empire. Each department had representatives throughout the empire who carried out the decisions made by Kubilai.

New Capitals

To house his new government, Kubilai designated two capitals. The summer capital at

In 1260 Kubilai Khan established the Yuan dynasty in China. Critics berated the khan for adopting the sedentary lifestyle of the Chinese.

Shang-tu was a city of three concentric walled compounds known as the Outer City, the Imperial City, and the Palace City. The Chinese architect Liu Ping-Chung designed Kubilai's capital as a series of concentric squares, with each side of a square facing one of the four points of the compass. Eight Buddhist monasteries were constructed in the eight corners of the city—at the four compass points and at the four midpoints between them. These eight monasteries reflected the eight trigrams of the Chinese book of divination known as the *I Ching*. Kubilai copied the design for his main capital at Ta-tu, in what is now Beijing. Construction at Ta-tu began in 1266. The interior compound at Ta-tu was home to Kubilai and his court, while the next compound housed government officials. Everyone else—ordinary citizens—lived beyond this wall in the open city. There were also yurts for members of the royal family scattered outdoors beside the city's lakes and gardens. In deference to his Mongol background, Kubilai's quarters were also designed to look like the inside of a traditional Mongol yurt and were hung with rugs.

With the purposeful segregation of classes within these compounds, Kubilai had established a hierarchy. Gone were the days of Genghis Khan, in which even the nobles lived basically the same lifestyle as the ordinary Mongol. Whereas Genghis had tried to spread his wealth among all his supporters, the steady accumulation of wealth in the hands of the upper classes had altered the fundamental nature of Mongol society, and many of the wealthier among them could no longer call themselves nomads. The court of Kubilai Khan became a pleasure palace where the aristocracy were not so much marked by military skill, as in Genghis's day, but by wealth alone.

Marco Polo, a Venetian merchant, visited the court of Kubilai Khan at Ta-tu and described the city as being,

> full of fine mansions, inns, and dwelling-houses. All the way down the sides of every main street there are booths and shops of every sort. All the building sites throughout the city are square and measured by the rule; and on every site stand large and spacious mansions with ample courtyards and gardens. These sites are allotted to heads of households, so that one belongs to such-and-such a person, representing such-and-such a family, the next to a representative of another family, and so all the way along.[43]

Opening Up the Chinese Economy

One of the greatest features of Ta-tu was the Grand Canal. The brainchild of Kubilai, this 136-mile canal was built by the hands of three million laborers. It linked Ta-tu in northern China with southern China and the Yangtze River, facilitating the shipment of grain within the country and helping to unite the two regions. Kubilai was genuinely concerned with improving China, and the canal was part of his plan to revitalize the Chinese economy. Soon after its completion, Ta-tu became a bustling inland port. To promote trade, Kubilai encouraged the development of merchant associations and helped to sponsor merchant expeditions. Kubilai introduced the use of paper money and insisted that all merchants wishing to trade in China exchange their gold and silver for

The Nomads Turn to Luxury

Genghis Khan refused a life of luxury and disliked elaborate social distinctions that elevated him above his countrymen. However, his successors grew more accustomed to wealth and aristocratic lifestyles, as evidenced by this description of the court of Kubilai Khan, from Marco Polo's Travels.

"When the Great Khan is holding court, the seating at banquets is arranged as follows. He himself sits at a much higher table than the rest at the northern end of the hall, so that he faces south. His principal wife sits next to him on the left. On the right, at a somewhat lower level, sit his sons in order of age, Chingiz the eldest being placed rather higher than the rest, and his grandsons and his kinsmen of the imperial lineage. They are so placed that their heads are on a level with the Great Khan's feet. Next to them are seated the other noblemen at other tables lower down again. And the ladies are seated on the same plan. All the wives of the Khan's sons and grandsons and kinsmen are seated on his left at a lower level, and next to them the wives of his nobles and knights lower down still. And they all know their appointed place in the lord's plan. The tables are so arranged that the Great Khan can see everything, and there are a great many of them. But you must not imagine that all the guests sit at table; for most of the knights and nobles in the hall take their meal seated on carpets for want of tables. Outside the hall the guests at the banquet number more than 40,000. For they include many visitors with costly gifts, men who come from strange countries bringing strange things, and some who have held high office and aspire to further advancement. Such are the guests who attend on such occasions, when the Great Khan is holding court or celebrating a wedding."

paper money issued by the government. The government could then hoard gold and silver as a ready source of capital for future military expeditions. This practice was later taken up by the western *ulus.*

Both land and sea trade flourished under Kubilai's rule, and European merchants, such as Marco Polo and his father Niccolo, began to visit China. Kubilai encouraged the export of Chinese products such as ceramics, silk, pearls, sugar, and rice, and a merchant fleet of ships was built to sell these wares along the coast of southeast Asia and in the Persian Gulf. Ceramics from the Yuan period, which broke with classical Chinese tradition and were decorated with innovative designs, became very popular abroad.

Kubilai promoted the work of Chinese artists and commissioned many beautiful horse paintings and sculptures. Physicians were also encouraged by Kubilai, who built hospitals and a medical academy. Following Kubilai's interest in the arts and sciences, Hulagu constructed an observatory in Persia. In turn, Kubilai invited Hulagu's Persian astronomers to his capital so they might build similar instruments there.

A Mongol Navy

Despite Kubilai's enlightened rule in China, the Sung continued to rebel against the Mongols. The Sung raised a fleet and the adversaries fought several naval battles from 1275 to 1276. Though better riders than sailors, the Mongols quickly mastered naval warfare and defeated the enemy vessels. On land the Sung forces were defeated with the help of

The Polos—well-known European merchants and travelers—kneel before Kubilai Khan, whose reign opened trade between the East and West. Brothers Niccolo and Maffeo Polo, along with Niccolo's son Marco, left Venice in 1271 to travel to the court of Kubilai Khan.

Persian siege engineers, whom Kubilai borrowed from his brother Hulagu.

Both during and after his quelling of the Sung rebellion in 1279, Kubilai, in a fit of expansionism, made two unsuccessful attempts to invade Japan in 1274 and 1281. Both times, storms and high winds prevented the forces from landing on the island of Japan, and thousands of soldiers were drowned. The Japanese attributed this luck to kamikaze, or "divine winds," protecting them.

Chinese Independence

Kubilai was never able to recover the success he had achieved in his youth, and his old age became filled with disappointment. After the death of his wife, Chabi, and the death of one of his sons, Kubilai became a recluse and began to drink and eat to excess. By 1294 he was dead, and his empire crumbled with him. Kubilai's son Temur succeeded him as Great Khan and

Kubilai Khan Creates a Flourishing International Trade

Kubilai Khan's efforts to promote commerce between China and the rest of the world resulted in an unprecedented volume of trade, as described here by Robert Marshall in Storm from the East.

"Though the end of Khubilai's reign was clouded by military and personal disappointments, his singular success in reuniting China would alone have guaranteed his position as one of the great figures in world history. However, it might also be argued that by continuing the policies of his grandfather to their logical conclusion—by internationalizing the empire—Khubilai made an even greater contribution to world history. . . . Chinese insularity was swept aside by a flood of foreign visitors come to the seat of the Great Khan. Khubilai's merchant fleet developed important markets in India, Sri Lanka, Malaya, and Java; and, because of the close links with the Ilkhanate, it also ventured as far west as the Persian Gulf, contributing to the growth of the new port of Ormuz.

Arab dhows [ships] also sailed east and became regular visitors at the ports of Hangchow, Quinsay and Zaiton. . . . Chinese manufactures reached everywhere under the custody of Mongol world dominance, and for the first time in human history Europe had direct contact with Cathay [China], through trade. Merchants traveled the vast Mongol highways from the Crimea, through the land of the Golden Horde to Sarai and Utrar, across the Altai Mountains and into the empire of the Great Khan, to Ta-tu."

The great fleet of Kubilai Khan, which was used to defeat the Sung rebellion in 1275 and 1276.

attempted to maintain control over China, but he had even less support from the other khans than his father had enjoyed, and the Chinese resistance to the Mongols had grown strong.

By the 1330s the rule of Kubilai's successors, peasant rebellions, famine, and the flooding of the Yellow River had thrown China into disarray. A peasant named Chu-Yuan-chang led a rebel movement that ousted the Mongols, and a new Chinese dynasty, the Ming, marked a return to self-rule in China. The Ming also began constructing the Great Wall to prevent another Mongol invasion of China.

The Collapse of the Mongol Khanates

Similar problems plagued the other Mongol *ulus.* Hulagu's Persian Ilkhanate was

Timur the lame (center), the last of the great Mongol leaders, is accompanied by Indian soldiers during a hunt. The Golden Horde collapsed after Timur's death in 1405.

succeeded by a series of Islamicized Mongols who were more sympathetic to the Persians. The last of these rulers, Abu Sa'id, produced no heir, and by 1335 the Ilkhanate was finished and Persia reverted back to local control. Mongol power remained concentrated longest not in the urban, sophisticated centers of Persia and China, but in central Asia and Russia. Gradually, the Mongol khans began to convert from shamanism to the faiths of their subjects, particularly Islam. Batu Khan's western territory, the Golden Horde, adopted Islam as the state religion in the early 1300s. At the same time, the Turkic language began to replace Mongolian as the spoken language of the ruling class.

The Remnants of an Empire

The last great representative of Mongol strength and tenacity—Timur the lame, or Tamerlane, as he became known in Western literature—rose to power around 1350. In a manner similar to Genghis Khan, Timur cultivated his following. Timur was descended from the Mongols, but he had been raised in the city and was a Turkic Muslim. He created an army based on Mongol military principles and conducted plundering raids in central Asia and the Middle East that rivaled the destruction of Genghis Khan. Timur died in 1405 on the way to China, which he was planning to conquer. He appointed no heir or administration to succeed him, and the Golden Horde collapsed shortly after his death. The last remaining piece of the Golden Horde, in the Crimea, lasted until that region was annexed by Russia's Catherine the Great in the late 1700s.

The Chagadei khanate in central Asia survived into the sixteenth century on the reputation of Genghis Khan, who had had great influence in the region. But in the early 1500s, Babur, a prince of Transoxiana and a descendant of both Genghis and Timur, fled to India to escape the Ozbeg Turks. He founded the Moghul dynasty (Moghul is the Persian pronunciation of Mongol) by conquering the northern Indian royal families. Babur's Moghul dynasty built the Taj Mahal, a piece of monumental architecture that remains an unlikely legacy of a nomad past.

In the late fourteenth and fifteenth centuries several different Mongol tribal leaders made attempts to reconquer China, but they lacked the necessary leadership. Mongolia had split between the two major tribal groups, the Oirats in the west and the Khalkhas in the east. The Oirats succeeded in capturing the Ming emperor about 1450, but they chose to ransom him rather than lead a campaign of conquest. The Oirats went on to dominate central Asia until they were beaten by an army of the Manchu dynasty in 1758. At this time, Mongolia was carved into the divisions that separate it today. The regions south of the Gobi Desert were taken by China, while northern Mongolia came under Russian control. Today, southern Mongolia, called the Inner Mongolian Autonomous Region, remains under Chinese control, but since the collapse of the U.S.S.R., northern Mongolia has become independent. The Mongolian independence movement found a symbol for freedom in the portrait of Genghis Khan. By invoking their illustrious past and rallying around the accomplishments of their ancestors, Mongolians have found a basis for their statehood today.

Legacies of the Mongols

The Mongols are most often remembered for their military power. Genghis Khan conquered more territory than any other individual in world history, yet in the Western world he has never enjoyed the status of other empire-builders like Napoleon or Alexander the Great. He is remembered for being a great destroyer rather than for the more positive achievements of his empire. But the legacies of the Mongols are manifold.

The law and order that Genghis Khan introduced to the steppe during his unification of the tribes transformed the Mongols from a feuding society into a powerful nation that became a major international player. The lives of average Mongols, and in some cases, those of the citizenry in conquered areas, were vastly improved by the changes that Genghis Khan's leadership and code of laws brought about.

Trade flourished under the Mongol Empire, and skilled workers from China, Persia, and elsewhere were brought to Mongolia to improve the Mongols' knowledge and develop their country. The Mongols constructed roads, patrolled them to keep them safe, and encouraged merchants to trade in their realm. These efforts increased the flow of goods east and west, as well as the exchange of ideas. The Chinese were introduced to Persian medicine and astronomy, while Persia was, in turn, enhanced by a knowledge of Chinese arts and sciences.

But just as goods and ideas traveled from one end of the world to the other, so did Mongol armies. The Mongol conquest of central Asia and Persia had damaging consequences for the culture of Islam. Many cities, and their populations, infrastructures, libraries, and treasures, were destroyed. Twentieth-century military historians consider the Mongol military a prototype for the modern military force of tanks and artillery, and during World War II both German Field Marshal Erwin Rommel and U.S. General George Patton admired the Mongol military's discipline and strategic brilliance. Genghis Khan's policy of developing an army based on personal following became the model for all nomad states. His policy of promotion within the army, based on personal merit rather than social status, was also novel for the Middle Ages.

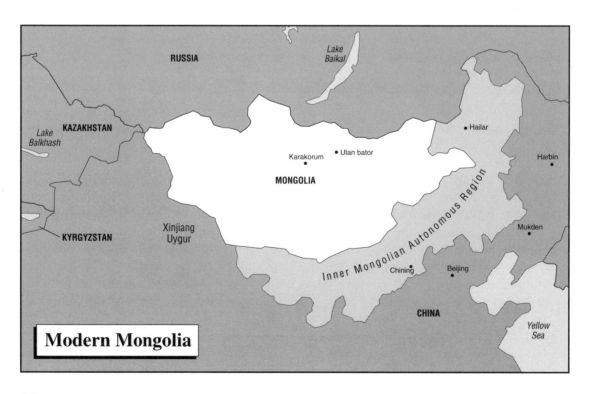

Modern Mongolia

Perhaps the most potent legacy of the Mongols stemmed from 1345, as the army of the Golden Horde was besieging the city of Kaffa on the Black Sea. A mysterious disease struck the Mongol army, decimating their ranks. Rather than simply give up the siege and retreat, the Mongol commander catapulted the corpses of his men over the city walls and allowed the disease to do the rest. This may have been the first recorded instance of biological warfare. The disease ravaged the city of Kaffa and spread, via merchants, to the Mediterranean and into Europe, where it ultimately reached as far as Greenland. This plague, known as the Black Death, killed one in three of the European population, exacting a toll that rivaled the destruction of any army.

Both aggressors and innovators, the Mongols left an enduring legacy of technology, cultural exchange, and conquest. Spreading knowledge as well as destruction, the Mongols succeeded in bridging social, religious, and scientific gaps between diverse populations. Their achievements, both military and cultural, earned the fear and respect of millions and permitted a tribe of nomads to rule a continent.

Notes

Chapter 1: The Nine-Tongued People

1. Quoted in Christopher Dawson, ed., *Mission to Asia*. Toronto: University of Toronto Press, 1980, p. 16.

2. Quoted in Dawson, *Mission to Asia*, pp. 16–17.

3. Quoted in Dawson, *Mission to Asia*, p. 7.

4. Quoted in Dawson, *Mission to Asia*, p. 18.

5. Quoted in Dawson, *Mission to Asia*, p. 103.

6. Quoted in Francis Woodman Cleaves, trans. and ed., *The Secret History of the Mongols*. Cambridge, MA: Harvard University Press, 1982, p. 254.

7. Quoted in Paul Ratchnevsky, *Genghis Khan: His Life and Legacy*. Trans. Thomas Nivison Haining. Cambridge, MA: Blackwell, 1991, pp. 13–14.

Chapter 2: Out of Nowhere: The Rise of the Mongols

8. Ratchnevsky, *Genghis Khan*, p. 28.

9. Quoted in Cleaves, *The Secret History*, pp. 76–77.

10. Quoted in Cleaves, *The Secret History*, p. 78.

11. Quoted in Cleaves, *The Secret History*, p. 96.

12. Ratchnevsky, *Genghis Khan*, p. 34.

13. Quoted in Ratchnevsky, *Genghis Khan*, p. 36.

14. Quoted in Ata-Malik Juvaini, *The History of the World Conqueror*, vol. 1. Trans. J. A.

Boyle. Cambridge, MA: Harvard University Press, 1958, p. 39.

15. Quoted in Cleaves, *The Secret History*, p. 113.

16. Quoted in Ratchnevsky, *Genghis Khan*, p. 40.

17. Cleaves, *The Secret History*, p. 123.

18. Quoted in Ratchnevsky, *Genghis Khan*, p. 86.

19. Ratchnevsky, *Genghis Khan*, p. 87.

Chapter 3: Building a Nation

20. Quoted in Dawson, *Mission to Asia*, pp. 32–33.

21. Robert Marshall, *Storm from the East: From Genghis Khan to Kubilai Khan*. Berkeley: University of California Press, 1993, pp. 40–41.

22. Quoted in Ratchnevsky, *Genghis Khan*, p. 187.

23. Quoted in Ratchnevsky, *Genghis Khan*, p. 149.

24. Quoted in Jim Stanfield, "Genghis Khan," *National Geographic*, December 1996, p. 9.

25. Quoted in Marshall, *Storm from the East*, p. 50.

26. Quoted in Juvaini, *The History of the World Conqueror*, vol. 1, pp. 80–81.

Chapter 4: Expanding the Empire

27. Marshall, *Storm from the East*, p. 53.

28. Juvaini, *The History of the World Conqueror*, vol. 1, p. 103.

29. Marshall, *Storm from the East*, pp. 53–54.

30. Juvaini, *The History of the World Conqueror*, vol. 1, p. 24.

31. Quoted in Dawson, *Mission to Asia,* p. xii.

32. Juvaini, *The History of the World Conqueror,* vol. 1, pp. 163–64.

33. Quoted in Marshall, *Storm from the East,* p. 61.

34. Marshall, *Storm from the East,* p. 88.

Chapter 5: East Meets West

35. Mary Hull, *The Travels of Marco Polo.* San Diego: Lucent Books, 1995, p. 18.

36. Quoted in Marshall, *Storm from the East,* p. 134.

37. Quoted in Marshall, *Storm from the East,* p. 135.

38. Quoted in Dawson, *Mission to Asia,* pp. 84–86.

39. Quoted in Dawson, *Mission to Asia,* p. 93.

40. Quoted in Dawson, *Mission to Asia,* p. 195.

Chapter 6: The Fracturing of Empire

41. Quoted in Marshall, *Storm from the East,* p. 181.

42. Quoted in Marshall, *Storm from the East,* p. 185.

43. Ronald Latham, trans. and ed., *The Travels of Marco Polo.* London: Penguin Books, 1958, pp. 128–29.

For Further Reading

Marlene Targ Brill, *Mongolia.* Chicago: Childrens Press, 1992. Provides a brief overview of Mongolia past and present, describing the geography, history, culture, industry, and people. This book also offers interesting photographs.

Robert Marshall, *Storm from the East: From Genghis Khan to Kubilai Khan.* Berkeley: University of California Press, 1993. Entertaining account of the origins and rise of the Mongols.

Michael Prawdin, *The Mongol Empire.* New York: Macmillan, 1940. An extensive history of the Mongols, beginning with the rise of Genghis Khan and concluding with the legacy of the Mongols to Asia. For those who want to know more about the Mongols and their empire, this is an excellent source.

Paul Ratchnevsky, *Genghis Khan: His Life and Legacy.* Trans. Thomas Nivison Haining. Cambridge, MA: Blackwell, 1991. This authoritative biography of Genghis Khan details the unification of the tribes and Genghis's rise to power in a very readable format.

Works Consulted

D. S. Benson, *The Mongol Campaigns in Asia*. Chicago: Bookmasters, 1991. Overview of Mongol military campaigns. A study of Mongol aggression, the book contains maps and details of the Mongol military campaigns of the thirteenth century.

James Chambers, *The Devil's Horsemen: The Mongol Invasion of Europe*. New York: Atheneum, 1979. European perspective on the history and effects of the Mongol invasion of eastern Europe.

Francis Woodman Cleaves, trans. and ed., *The Secret History of the Mongols*. Cambridge, MA: Harvard University Press, 1982. Part myth, part history, this manuscript was commissioned by the Mongol government upon the death of Genghis Khan.

Christopher Dawson, ed., *Mission to Asia*. Toronto: University of Toronto Press, 1980. A collection of travel accounts published by various missionaries to the Mongols, including William of Rubruck and Giovanni of Plano Carpini.

Herodotus, *The Histories*. Baltimore: Penguin Books, 1960. Greek history with references to Asia and an astonishing array of facts, legends, and digressions about the geography and culture of the rest of the known world.

Michel Hoang, *Genghis Khan*. New York: New Amsterdam, 1990. A study of the man and myth of Genghis Khan. The book also provides the views of the Europeans and Middle Easterners who came into contact with the Mongols.

Mary Hull, *The Travels of Marco Polo*. San Diego: Lucent Books, 1995. An account of the journeys of the Polo family across Asia and their stay at the court of Kubilai Khan.

Ata-Malik Juvaini, *The History of the World Conqueror*. Vols. 1 and 2. Trans. John Andrew Boyle. Cambridge, MA: Harvard University Press, 1958. The story of the Mongol conquest of western Asia told by a historian in the Muslim tradition. Juvaini wrote his history at the Mongol court and lyrically describes the events that transpired.

Ronald Latham, trans. and ed., *The Travels of Marco Polo*. London: Penguin Books, 1958. Account of the Venetian traveler Marco Polo's journey to Asia and his stay at the court of Kubilai Khan.

D. J. Levy, *Chinese Narrative Poetry: The Late Han Through T'ang Dynasties*. Durham, NC: Duke University Press, 1988. Translations by the author, including "Eighteen Songs of a Nomad Flute" by Cai Yan, a Hsiung-nu abductee.

Beatrice Forbes Manz, *The Rise and Rule of Tamerlane*. Cambridge, MA: Cambridge University Press, 1989. Examines Tamerlane's rule and the synthesis of Turco-Mongolian and Islamic tradition, including its impact on the Ottoman, Mughal, and Safavid Empires.

Bertold Spuler, *The Mongol Period: History of the Muslim World.* Princeton, NJ: Markus Wiener Publishers, 1994. History of the Mongols and the Islamic countries with which they came in contact.

Jim Stanfield, "Genghis Khan," *National Geographic*, December 1996. A journalist's trip through central and eastern Asia brings him into contact with the region's historic past as part of the Mongol Empire.

H. G. Wells, *The Outline of History.* Vol. 2. New York: Garden City Publishing, 1930. Condenses thousands of years of history into two volumes, but offers much commentary on the Mongol military.

Malcolm Yapp, *Chingis Khan and the Mongol Empire.* San Diego: Greenhaven Press, 1980. A children's source book of documents pertaining to the history of the Mongols.

Index

Picture Credits

Cover photo: Giraudon/Art Resource, NY

AKG London, 34, 36, 40, 54, 56

Archive Photos, 50

© J. M. Bertrand/Explorer/Photo Researchers, 26

Bibliothèque Nationale, 62

The Bodleian Library, Oxford, MS. Bodl. 264, fol. 220r, 91

© Dean Conger/Corbis, 17

Corbis-Bettmann, 29, 30, 52, 68, 71, 93, 94

© George Holton/Photo Researchers, 14, 64

© Landau/Photo Researchers, 15

Library of Congress, 70

The Metropolitan Museum of Art, Purchase, Bequest of Dorothy Graham Bennett, 1993, 66

North Wind Picture Archives, 11, 87

Jeff Paris, 45

Stock Montage, Inc., 16, 21, 43, 58, 75, 88

© Brian Vikander/Corbis, 33

© Elisabeth Weiland/Photo Researchers, 24

Werner Forman/Art Resource, NY, 47, 84

© Nik Wheeler/Corbis, 65

About the Author

Mary Hull has a B.A. in history from Brown University. She is a free-lance writer and lives in Boston, where she writes for educational publishers and businesses. In 1997 her book *Struggle and Love* was chosen by the New York Public Library Association as one of the best books of the year for teenagers.